Hey,

Thank you so much for your support.

REAL ESTATE
MASTERY

It's time to make moves

Jessica

itsjessicamyers.com

Real Estate Mastery

by Jessica Myers

Deal MKR Publishing

Real Estate Mastery
© 2022 by Jessica Myers

Deal MKR Publishing
Atlanta, Georgia

All rights reserved solely by the author. The author guarantees all contents are original and do not infringe upon the legal rights of any other person or work. No part of this book may be reproduced in any form without the permission of the author.

ISBN-13: 979-8-218-0799-8-7

LCCN: 2022918534

DEDICATION

I would not be here if it were not for my family and circle of close friends that have encapsulated me and surrounded me with their love and support.

I would like to dedicate this book to my family. To my parents Janice and Greg, grandparents, sister and brother, and most importantly, OTP (you know who you are).

Without your investment into my life, I would not have had the courage to BE. Thank you for your love and support through the journey I call life.

To Ms. Sylvia High and the entire Aiming High Family, thank you for encouraging me to live full out. It is because of you and your training and encouragement that I stand today with power, boldness, and courage!

Table of Contents

Foreword by Jullien Gordon..........................ix
Introduction..xv

Chapter 1
What Real Estate Did for Me..........................1

Chapter 2
What Can Real Estate Do for You?....................7

Chapter 3
Different Players in Real Estate.....................13

Chapter 4
Build Your Criteria..................................23

Chapter 5
Building Your Dream Team...........................43

Chapter 6
The Art of the Deal.................................63

Chapter 7
Making Offers.......................................85

Chapter 8
Working with Contractors 95

Chapter 9
Making Money 103

Chapter 10
Failure Is an Option 111

Chapter 11
Growing Your Empire 119

Chapter 12
Conclusion 135

Contract Templates 139

Foreword

I am honored and delighted to write this foreword, not only because Jessica Myers has been a friend and real estate colleague for a few years now, but also because I believe deeply in the educational value of empowering real estate investors and entrepreneurs, especially amongst minorities and women. I also believe that real estate, if played right, is the key to financial freedom. No matter the level or stage a person is entering, they can educate themselves by learning the skills, key fundamentals, practices and steps presented in this book.

There are 4 classes of people in The United States. The three that most people know include the lower class, middle class, and upper class. But there is a fourth class that the wealthy belong to called the asset class. Those in the asset class are the only group of people that are truly free. And you will find that almost everyone in the asset class owns real estate beyond their primary residence.

You enter the asset class when your assets, particularly real estate, create passive income that exceeds your monthly cost of living.

Jessica and I both became part of the asset class thanks to real estate. And we also share a passion for giving back and teaching our community what we've learned along the way. There are those who practice real estate but don't teach. And then there are those who teach real estate but don't practice. It is rare to find someone like Jessica or myself who loves both.

Over the past few years my Multifamily Movement has helped over 400 people acquire their first multifamily home and achieve rent and mortgage freedom. That means that they will never pay for housing for the rest of their life. Together, my students have acquired over $1.5 million dollars in real state nationwide. Our big hairy audacious goal is 3,000 closings on over $1 billion dollars of real estate in the next 5 years.

This mission can only be achieved when leaders like Jessica rise to the occasion. When experts like myself and Jessica share our knowledge and normalize regular discussion amongst friends, family and the culture around real estate, the more people see and understand its incredible power and value. People want more for themselves and their families. They want security and

Foreword

most of all, the freedom to live and do walk in their God-given purpose daily without worrying about money.

I was first introduced to Jessica Myers when she attended my 2-day money mindset event in Atlanta. From there, she joined my high-level coaching program to expand her vision and multiply her value. Being that my mission is to help people get "free" through real estate, I was inspired by Jessica's passion and natural ability to connect, break down information that is foreign and intimidating to many people and deliver in a way that is highly informative and easily digestible.

Jessica's hands-on, in the field masterclass, a one-on-one coaching program and hosts The Deal MKR Fireside Chat, a multi-city networking event that tours across the country to educate and bring together future investors, entrepreneurs and investors are all a part of that vision. And now this book caps it off by summarizing and simplifying the vast amount of knowledge Jessica possesses. I used to say that real estate couldn't be taught in a book, just like reading a Gordon Ramsey recipe book doesn't mean you can cook. But Jessica has successfully managed to write this book in a way where you feel like you are walking side-by-side with her on an actual construction site making it a perfect introduction to the real estate game before you participate is one of her more immersive learning experiences.

Jessica is a pioneer in our community. She has studied, explored and mastered areas of real estate, from wholesaling to hotels to fundraising and new construction. Not to mention she is also one of the country's first and youngest black female owners of a major hotel chain, an author and now co-producer and host of her own television show, Real Estate Mastery with Jessica Myers on the HOPE TV Network.

In this book, Jessica has produced a powerful tool for those who are serious about the real estate game by highlighting the 7 players. In her opening chapter, she lets us in on her backstory and how a moment of accolade at the age of twenty-two as a sales rep at CBS in NYC was the "Ah Ha" moment she needed to move into another direction which ultimately led her to real estate.

This book is for those who want to win in real estate. This book is for the ones who are determined to break free of the bounds of corporate and own their own time. This book is for the men and women who have capital but don't know how to find the right deal. This book is for you if you need to learn how to build your team. It's for you if you want to leave a legacy of generational wealth and for those who need a complete mind shift and education in real estate. In short, Jessica's book offers the blueprint for your real estate success.

Foreword

Reading this book, you will find that you don't have to have been born into money or have majored in business and finance to be successful at real estate. You can be form the upper class, middle class, or lower class, a doctor or a bus driver, you can be twenty two or sixty two, have three degrees or none and still make it happen. You will also find that this book will be hard to put down once you start and if you follow it and take ownership of its content and apply, you will definitely reap the rewards. Your mental real estate, the space between the temples on your forehead, is the most important real estate to own first and this book will get your mind right. From there, owning physical real estate in inevitable.

Abundance is your birthright. God's first gift to man before life was real estate. As Jessica always says…You know you got it, Let's get it, Let's go!!!!

Jullien Gordon
Mr. Multifamily
Leader of The Multifamily Movement
Real estate investor, educator, and developer
www.MultifamilyMovement.com

Introduction

I'm normally shy, but I know that about myself, so with my awareness, I'm always putting myself in uncomfortable situations. But within that un-comfortability comes growth and change, only if you choose it to. Knowing that I'm shy, I've intentionally gone to career days over the past ten years to practice connecting and engaging with audiences. Trust me, if you can't connect, no one will tell you quicker than a twelve-year-old kid.

Understanding that about myself and finding ways to work around that is how I've been able to achieve success. It is identifying the areas of weakness and strengthening them, just as you would go to the gym to workout. It is NOT always easy, but it is always worth it.

A mentor of mine once said, "There is no such thing as a one-sided pancake. Everything that is good is bad, and everything that is bad is good." What does that mean? When you ask for patience, patience doesn't just rest on your lap. You will go through some tough situations that teach you the principles of patience. You will endure pain to get the glory. Much of the success from the lessons I've learned have been through the lens of many failures. But I've transmuted that failure, gotten back up, performed an autopsy on the situation, and used it to empower me to do greater.

On the flip side, there are many good things that may happen that do not put us into the best of situations. I'm sure we've all been there before—seeing something great but had negative consequences or reactions in the end. I know I have.

In this experience we call life, embracing the duality of both good and bad will allow you to have a fuller experience. If you feel insecure or shy about talking about wealth, that is ok, but don't stay there. It's complex because your currency is your life's report card, the true tail sign of how effective and impactful you've been with the decisions you've made to the best of your ability. No one desires to see bad grades, but unless you have a mechanism to measure success, you won't even realize where you are. Understanding key economic financial principles is like going to a study group to get your grades up. The more you study, the better your grades.

Introduction

As a professional with experience in sales, marketing, and grass root development strategy, a question I am often asked is, "Why are you in real estate?" My response is always, "Why not real estate?!" Thinking inside of the box gets you what you already have and keeps you within your comfort zone. I love to surround myself with trailblazers and innovators, and one thing I have quickly learned from them is that investment opportunities are the vehicles needed to help you accomplish your life goals!

Where do you want to be ten years from now? Wait, why is that always a question? Where do you want to be sixty days from now? Are you striving for financial independence? Do you have business ideas you can't wait to launch? Or maybe you are saving money to put your kids through college. Perhaps you already have your eyes set on a beach where you want to spend your golden retirement years. Wherever you are right now on life's notorious cycles, whatever dreams you hold in your heart, you can prepare to live it. See yourself in the future. The immediate future! The right avenue and opportunity should not take a decade to manifest. When you have the wisdom, tools, resources, and support all aligned, you can enjoy the fruits of your labor sooner. This book, along with the workbook, will guide you to realize your dreams!

I love a good self-help motivational book. I have written a few myself! Tangible wisdom and call-to-action items you can actually implement in real life will bring you more value than any speech, affirmation, or ten-step guide that I can possibly teach. There is beauty teaching another to fish, and I am thrilled to share my success and lessons with you.

Make this book your own! Write in it, plan in it, dream in it, highlight in it (like a rainbow), carry it into meetings, close deals with it in your hands, learn, grow, profit, and repeat. I have intentionally left space at the end of each chapter for you to write down your thoughts. I believe in uplifting others and that there is enough success to go around. Therefore, there is no need to hoard information. In this book, I have tried to share with you my most trusted advice and lessons in real estate. I am personally rooting for you, wishing you infinitely unmeasurable success.

Let's begin!

CHAPTER 1

WHAT REAL ESTATE DID FOR ME

Twenty million five hundred thousand dollars! That's the dollar value of real estate I have transacted as of 2021, and that number is steadily climbing. If you had asked me if I dreamed of hitting that number before my thirtieth birthday, I would've laughed. Don't get me wrong, I have always been a go-getter. I was hustling key chains and candy to pay for my school trips in high school and developing business plans when I was in middle school. Despite my hustling ways, growing up in the suburbs of Atlanta, I had no idea that I would pursue a career in real estate.

My first "real" job was as an intern at Fox 5 in Atlanta, Georgia. By the time I was twenty-two, I had climbed that corporate ladder and was serving as a sales rep for CBS in NYC. I was doing well and had pretty good success, yet something was missing. One day, toward the end of the year, I requested time off. I had a vacation planned for the Bahamas. I performed as a hardworking employee, yet my request was denied. I found myself talking to my supervisor about the dilemma. This is the advice I received: "Well, the only solution we have is borrowing vacation days from next year." Wait, what? That solution had hit me like a lightning bolt. I learned that I did not own my time. In fact, the company owned my time. It suddenly became absurd to me that I had to borrow time from my future. That made me start thinking, *How could I buy back my own time?*

After returning from my vacation (because I still went), I found myself sitting at a table across from one of the company's executives. They were thanking me for my commitment with a plaque celebrating five years with the company. Directly across from me, at the same table, was a man getting the same plaque, only his said twenty-five years. In that moment, I realized that this could be me in twenty years. Another twenty years, and I would still be at the same table. That realization, combined with my dad telling me I was climbing the corporate ladder—the ladder was possibly on the wrong wall—I further realized I was meant for more.

What Real Estate Did For Me

Looking back, I am glad for my time in CBS. I had learned many lessons. First, I learned how to communicate with others. Being a broadcasting network, everything at CBS is about how to connect with people and communicate clearly. Second, I learned what I didn't want to be. I had thought that this was the career path that I wanted. That meeting celebration of five years of time was an eye-opener for me. I was very blessed to discover that this was not the career for me before I had wasted any more of my life chasing the "corporate American dream."

The next few years were very interesting. After spending some time soul-searching, I found myself at a real estate weekend class called Abundance Education. I had discovered their name on the internet and figured I would give it a try. At the end of the weekend, they took the students to a house, and we watched the real estate agent process. I had immediately fallen in love. I had found my new career.

Initially, I thought I might want to be a real estate agent; however, I found out about wholesaling and flipping. Additionally, I learned to quickly network and connected with a real estate group in Atlanta. Within a few months, I had bought my first house. Two months later, I had bought three more houses. I was so excited about my newfound career that I wanted to quit my job right then and there! I remember telling Joel, my husband, that I wanted to quit work and do real estate. He was supportive; but looking back, I think I sounded a little crazy!

Luckily, my boss was gracious with me. He asked me about my plan. so I told him I didn't know! I just knew I wanted to do real estate. He encouraged me to stay at least another year until I had a plan, and I did. His kind gesture helped me to pay the bills and get my nails done while I dabbled in real estate and learned the ropes. Eventually, though, I was getting in my own way. I realized that I was too comfortable. If I wanted to move forward in real estate, I would need to jump all in.

In 2016, about a year into my real estate journey, I hadn't made much progress. Yes, I had purchased a few properties and was living comfortably, but nothing was making any money yet. My only income came from my full-time job. That's when I changed. I started to make some sacrifices. I stopped traveling, canceled my nail and lashes appointments, and stopped my weekend shopping trips. I never really overspent in these categories, but I realized if I could save a few hundred dollars here and there, I would be able to invest more and see profits come back a lot sooner. I was so dedicated to saving money for investments that Joel and I moved in with my parents for about a year so we could save on rent. Between my job, his job as a software engineer, and saving on rent money, we saved much money and eventually saw our real estate journey go forward.

Fast forward a few more years. I am building a development in The Golden Isles here in Georgia, and our group has closed on a Home2Suites by Hilton Hotel in El Reno, OKC, along with our Stay Bridge and Hampton Inn in Indiana. We have been acknowledged by Forbes, Black Enterprise, and other media outlets for our work. I have coached thousands of students to start their own real estate journey. Additionally, I am laying the groundwork to develop real estate in Africa and around the world. I spend my time doing what I love, including developing real estate and traveling the world. Of course, your beginning may look different from mine. I've heard stories of people quitting their job, maxing out their credits for a down payment, and launching their real estate journey that way. I'm not necessarily advocating doing it that way. I am sharing how I was able to start investing in real estate while still working my nine-to-five job. What you do need to do is take the first step. No one has ever changed their life by staying in their comfort zone. Don't wait for the perfect deal; it doesn't exist. Create it!

CHAPTER 2

WHAT CAN REAL ESTATE DO FOR YOU?

The power of real estate is real. It changed my life, and I believe it can change the lives of anyone dedicated to learning how to invest in real estate. No, it is not easy, but nothing is. However, I don't think I am more stressed now than when I was working for corporate America. Yes, I have more responsibilities, but I also have more freedom. Yes, things go wrong, but they also go wrong at a regular nine-to-five job as well. No longer do I have to "borrow time." I now can buy my time.

Next, I want to share with you the lessons I learned and the experiences I endured. If you take this information and apply it, I promise, you will learn to buy back your time. Whether you want to make side change, become a millionaire, or become a billionaire, the principles remain the same.

What Makes a Good Real Estate Investor?

A lot has happened over the last few years. Since I bought my first property, my initial investment has grown over 100 percent, and I am constantly looking for ways to expand my portfolio. I've been blessed so much. Looking back, I realize that it wasn't always easy. Like I said earlier, during the first few years, I really didn't make money at all. I lost quite a bit on my first few deals. That's why it is important to have the proper mindset when going into real estate. Before diving into the specifics of how I have built a million-dollar real estate company, there are a few things you must realize about yourself. Indeed, there are many paths to success in real estate. Whether you are a wholesaler, flipper, or developer, there are many things to learn and understand about buying, selling, and ultimately making a profit. In addition to knowledge, I believe there are some shared traits that all real estate investors must have.

Resourcefulness

Growing up, my parents didn't have much money. We paid our bills and lived a comfortable life but didn't have extra money for many trips and vacations. Rather than get down on myself about my situation, I took action. Whenever a school trip would come around, I was ready. How? Using the resources I had. I sold keychains, candy, and built business plans and budgets so that I could meet my goals (going on school trips).

I carried this same mentality into real estate. I remember one of my first deals. We bought a property in Decatur, a suburb of Atlanta. The property was a five-bedroom, three-bathroom house. We bought it to flip, but the selling price wasn't what we wanted. We had done everything right except pay attention to one small detail. The house had a kitchen that was "below grade," a lower height than the rest of the house. That sounds small, but it became a big deal. Lenders are apparently less willing to lend money for a house with that setup. I still don't get it to this day, but that's part of real estate—understanding the rules of the game. Rather than be defeated and sell the house for a loss or very small profit, we thought outside the box. The house itself was great. It was close to the main road and decent shopping, so we turned the property into a short-term rental through Airbnb. Over the next year, we netted $60,000, which was more than what we asked on the flip!

Resilience

Real estate is always full of surprises. I spend much time creating plans and procedures to ensure that my deals go as smoothly as possible. We still run into issues. A few years ago, my partner and I decided to buy a million-dollar house. At this time, it would have been our first time doing this. Until then, I had never done more than a 2,000-square-feet area or more than a $350,000 purchase price. We were excited and decided not to wait on our lender to get started. Instead, we started with our own money. We were about $300,000 into the deal, which included tearing down the house and rebuilding, when he told us that he couldn't process a loan on a property with no house. What? Not all mortgage companies will serve a loan on land, so another lesson learned.

Over the next four months, we had to put our operations on hold. We spent that time searching for a lender who would finance this project. We could've given up, but we didn't. Finally, after six lenders turned us down, we found a private lender who funded our project. The house sold for $1,800,000, almost a million dollars more than we had anticipated! Many people would've given up as soon as a wrench was thrown in the plans. You can't do that in real estate. Being tough and resilient is part of the game.

Due Diligence

As a person who likes to move quickly, due diligence may be my least favorite part about real estate, but I've learned that it's the most important. One of my first deals was with a friend of mine. I was super excited about the deal and about working with a friend, and so was she. I didn't have an LLC, but she did, so we formed a partnership, and I naively went along with her without a contract. By the time the deal was ending, she had boxed me out of the project. I didn't get a penny from that deal. Luckily, she did pay back the lender, so I didn't get in trouble for that. Lesson: Cross your t's, dot your i's, and do things right. You will have people who want to betray you, or legal issues from a past sale may come up. In real estate, it is always wise to double check and be diligent. It's a headache, but it will save you many headaches when things come up.

Patience

As my examples above showed, I have had to wait for four months before a deal was able to be made, and I should have taken my time to do proper due diligence so I didn't get robbed. In fact, I still need patience. Deals take time. Making money in real estate takes time. This is not a get-rich-quick scheme. If I have a goal of making $83,000 a month in passive income, then I know I need to have a plan. There is no way that I can accomplish such a large goal like that in a short period of time. I can possibly speed up the process and be ambitious, but unless someone wants to just give me the money to do all those deals at once, it will take time. I'm fine with that. It's part of the fun, so whether you are trying to make a few thousand a month or a few million in a year, you need patience.

Risk-Taking

I ran into someone who was following me in 2017. Four years later, I ran into her again. I was excited to see what progress she had made. She told me she was still looking to get in the game. She knew all the stuff I knew. She had seen that I had changed my life by taking action, yet she still hadn't gotten started. She had spent several years looking for the perfect deal and had not gotten in the game. That's when I realized that I had gotten in because I was not looking for the perfect deal. I just knew that I needed to get in. I knew that I needed to take the risk.

My first deal was a risk. We had made our plans before realizing that our appraiser had made a typo. We planned to make a huge profit selling our house, but then we learned that the house was worth $252k, not $352k. Looking back, it doesn't matter. I learned the lesson to do my due diligence, I set parameters for my projects, and I never looked back. Risk-taking is in front of all of us. Of course, the first deal will cause you to learn, to act, and to start growing your connections. But you won't learn the lessons or build the connections you need to succeed unless you take a risk.

CHAPTER 3

Different Players in Real Estate

The opportunity of real estate is available to everyone. There are so many ways to be involved in real estate. If you want to sell houses, be a realtor. If you want to become a landlord, house-hack and rent out your basement. Even if you don't have the capital or desire to flip homes, you can wholesale. The beauty of real estate is in its assortment, yet the ultimate path to wealth in real estate is investing. Often, the best realtors become investors because they understand that investing is where you start to buy back your time. Before beginning the details of investing, I would like you to understand the different ways you can get started in real estate.

Active Investor — a person or organization that puts money into a business, property, or asset with the hope of making a profit. In real estate, an active investor is involved in the operations of their company; their investment is their time and money. With their team, they actively search for deals, often through networking. They build a legal team and accounting team to handle paperwork and contracts necessary to build out the strategy and vision of their company. An investor should be very good at handling stress, multitasking, and decision-making. Equally important is the ability to network and build strong business connections with other investors.

Passive Investor — a passive investor is the same as an active investor except they are not actively involved in the daily operations of the company. They may be busy with another company or job, possibly looking for an additional income source. Although they are not responsible for daily operations, they should take time to build connections with trustworthy business partners who will give them a return on their cash investment.

Wholesaler — someone who finds and purchases properties to immediately resell. These properties are often distressed and require extensive work. A wholesaler is not interested in doing the repairs but typically connects with an investor who is able to do that work. Although there is a slight markup in cost to the investor, the wholesaler saves them time and money by doing the legwork of searching out a deal. A wholesaler should have strong negotiating skills and a strong eye to see a good real estate potential. Stronger negotiating skills for purchase price will lead to more money for the sales price of the real estate.

Flipper — a property flipper shares many skills with a wholesaler. Both are very good at finding distressed properties and purchasing them for resale. The only difference is in renovations. Rather than turn it around for a quick profit, a property flipper will renovate and repair the house before selling it. This requires more capital but also allows for larger returns. A flipper must be skilled in estimating repair costs and able to build a strong team of contractors to do the repairs efficiently and economically.

Landlord — is typically an investor, but they do more work. Where an investor may purchase a property and hire a management team to rent it out, a landlord will purchase the property and handle all repairs, finding tenants, and any other issues that come up. This saves money and can be a good way to create cash flow using your property, but it takes much time. A landlord needs to have strong connections to repairmen and have good money management skills. The typical return on a property is in the hundreds, so excessive repairs and upgrades can consume your profits very quickly.

Bird-Dogging — You may have heard this term relating to hunting. What does hunting have to do with the real estate strategy of "bird-dogging"? It assumes that "the dog" is the investor, and the "bird" is the house in distress. The goal is to find a house that is being offered for a lower price than its former appraisal. This discount of sorts happens for various reasons: a house in foreclosure or an old house needing tremendous repair work. The bird-dog scouts a discounted property for the investors. The investor gets the property for a discounted price, renovates, and sells it for more than the purchase price. Since a scouter is not buying the property, there is no financial obligation. The scouter could get both a property finder fee as well a prospective buyer fee.

The ultimate path to wealth is by getting your money to work for you. That's why flipping and investing is a better long-term option for many people. However, whatever you choose, getting involved in real estate offers many potential benefits and perks that many other careers can't match.

Uncapped Earning Potential

Real estate is not a get-rich-quick scheme. I am repeating this because it is important to know and understand. I warn you, distance yourself from any person or opportunity promising you otherwise. Although you won't make money overnight, a real estate career is very lucrative. Your first year may yield a small profit. If you are a real estate agent while employed in another job, you may not see your maximum earning potential. If you are a passive investor investing $2,000–$10,000 per project, you, too, may not see the fullest return of your investment because, naturally, our return of investment is dependent on the size of the original investment. I could give you one hundred other scenarios as to why your experience in real estate could be less than impressive monetarily. But those are mostly exceptions. There is a high-earning potential; it is realistic and absolutely within reach. Just like in every industry, there is a wealth gap. Some people will earn little, some moderately, and some become incredibly wealthy doing what they love. Your level of involvement, learned wisdom, branding, networking, and the team of people with whom you align yourself with will directly affect your earning potential.

Possible Residual Income

Not everyone has the heart to be a landlord or property manager. Honestly, I have lived that life. It is really challenging and time-consuming. However, all the expenses, pleasing the renters, repairs, and everything else involved in the life of a landlord or property manager, there is the benefit of residual income. The first couple of years renting a property may not yield profit, but it's coming! Considering rental options?

Rental options include: traditional leases, Airbnb, or vacation rentals.

Expanded Networks

Real estate is a big industry with small circles. It is no secret that your network impacts your net worth! Don't be shy and embrace connecting with other like-minded, driven professionals. You are one connection away from your next business breakthrough. Real estate is a referral-based, personal business. Your networking involvement will connect you to all walks of life, open many doors, and give you access to priceless assets.

A Path to Financial Independence

Finance can be intimidating. As adults, we don't often know everything we need to know about managing money or training our money to work for us. Nationally, the majority of us are middle class, living a debt-free life, yet the concept of investing is often out of reach. But it doesn't have to be. Don't let the lack of education prevent you from finding the path of financial independence! Teach yourself. Being self-taught is always empowering. Financial literacy is within reach. You can live a life where you pay cash for your vacations, cars, and luxury items, and live mortgage free and send your kids to college without the help of a bank.

I didn't venture into real estate to become financially savvy . . . that part is a blessing I didn't even ask for! But in all my getting, I am getting understanding. The more networking tables I have sat at, the more investors I have pitched to, the more proposals I have written, and with every deal I have seen to completion, I have become more financially sound. I have grown to understand money. I have grown to understand markets and market trends. Finally, I can spot a good investment opportunity from a distance! I have self-taught, and I have learned! It is in me!

A Vehicle to Pursue Other Goals and Ventures

To the professional who has no interest in real estate investing, this is for you! You are passionate about another industry, and that is okay! You don't view real estate as your endgame. No problem. Whatever your endgame is, real estate can help get you there. In most cases, whatever role you have in this industry will be a self-managed role; you choose your hours, work location, have access to high earnings, and in return, you can fund your wildest dreams. Get excited!

Are you ready to do the work? Or maybe you are already an active investor or agent and ready to take your portfolio to the next level. Do it! There is no time like the present, and sometimes a little nudge is all it takes to encourage a leap of faith to pursue a new venture in real estate.

Have you ever looked at a map of a mall or subway and seen the little red dot indicating where you are located? This is your red dot. You are here. You are at the beginning of your real estate journey. There are many directions that real estate can lead you, but the only one viable to you is the one that reaches your destination. Don't get caught up in what you know, how much or how little you can invest, or what's waiting down the many other paths. Just start. Learn and grow along the way. Plan to fail. Plan to learn. Plan to win. There is no right time to start a venture; you just have to do it. Start.

After reading this, I suggest you take a good look at this list again and do some soul-searching. Of course, everyone likes the sound of passive investment. Who doesn't want to make "free" money? First, money isn't free. Whatever your job or career is now, it is paying for that investment. You are still putting time in somewhere. Second, are you able to afford losing that money? If not, passive investing may not be for you. Again, a landlord sounds amazing. Buying a house and putting in a long-term renter is great until it's not. Things go wrong, stuff breaks, and people sue. Are you ready to deal with the headache of having people in your property and being responsible for every little thing that goes wrong? Take time and determine what path is the best for you, your personality, and the lifestyle you want.

I love to travel, so I knew that whatever I did, it needed to allow me the flexibility to travel. Being an investor did that for me. What do you want to do? Think about that when you are considering your real estate path.

CHAPTER 4

BUILD YOUR CRITERIA

By now, you should have an idea of where you are and what path you want to take. Now, we need to look at how you want to invest. Whichever path you chose, you will need to understand these principles to succeed in real estate. So, let's get started! Once you have determined your course, it is time to build your criteria. Your criteria will do several things for you:

1. Protect you from making bad decisions;
2. Show you who you need to connect with; and
3. Show you what you need to learn.

Your criteria is essentially the beginnings of your business plan. Therefore, take your time and make sure you lay out your criteria clearly.

Reverse-Engineer Your Goal

Before you can figure anything else out, you must know what your goal is. Otherwise, you don't have a place to aim. My goal was to be a millionaire. More specifically, I wanted to earn a million dollars in cash flow a year. Doing the math, that means I had to earn $83,333.33/month. Whatever path I took, whatever properties I bought, it had to lead to this goal. Plus, I wanted to reach my goal and have the ability to travel. When I first started, I thought I just wanted to do wholesale and house flips. I knew that based on the average amount I was making from each flip, I would need to flip one thousand properties every year to reach my goal or diversify my strategies. This is where starting with your goal helps you to make better decisions. However you decide to invest in real estate, it has to start with an end in mind: your goal.

Capital

The first criteria you need to establish is capital. When I decided to enter real estate, I needed cash. I had some knowledge, natural skills, connections, and a desire to succeed, yet I wasn't getting anywhere without money. That's when I made the decision to partner with others who had access to money. Understanding which resources you have access to is a good starting point because you may have access to more than you think.

Build Your Criteria

Criteria for determining how much cash you need:

1. Down payment (typically a deal will need 20 percent of the value of the project);
2. Closing costs (you must pay attorneys, title fees, escrow, and other costs to finalize a deal, usually up to 5 percent of the final price);
3. Holding costs (mortgage, loan repayments, interest); and
4. Renovation costs (contractors, materials, etc.).

The average real estate investing deal generally requires $40,000 to $60,000. If you find a great deal, you may need less than that. But you will most likely want to find a way to raise at least that amount of capital. If you have the cash to cover the whole deal, you still have a decision to make. How much of that capital are you willing to invest? It may be a good idea to save that cash for another project. If you do not have the capital to get started, don't worry; there are other capital resources. For most of my deals, I either bring no money or only part of the money to the deal. I work to find money from many different sources like hard money lenders or a line of credit.

Hard money lenders are those who will give you cash outside of a financial institution. Typically, they are a group of private equity investors or hedge funds, and they loan money on short terms for an investment project. They typically look at your experience and the strength of a deal. Their interest rates will be higher than a bank, but they are able to get you cash more quickly than a bank. Whether you have no cash or need more cash, you can always find someone who does. Your job is to take inventory of how much you have and how much you need.

Time

The second criteria to consider is time. How much time do you need to reach your goals? How much of your time are you willing to put into your real estate investments? I remember when I started, I was prepared to make real estate my full-time job. I was ready to go all in. However, I still needed cash to live and finance my projects while I built my portfolio. For the first two years of my real estate journey, I had to balance working full-time with CBS in Atlanta and connecting with buyers and viewing properties on the weekend and after work. No, it's not ideal, but it's what I knew I needed to do to succeed. When looking at real estate, you must decide how much time you have to devote.

Build Your Criteria

Things to consider:

1. How involved can you be in the renovation project;
2. How much time can you spend looking for deals;
3. How much time can you spend on investing in a day; and
4. How much time do you want to spend away from work?

There are no one-size-fits-all answers to this. For me, I know I like to travel a lot. Therefore, I built travel into my work schedule. When I traveled to Exuma, Bahamas, I planned it around my real estate projects, but I also left time for enjoying the area. Honestly decide for yourself how much time you want to buy. For example, if I want to take a vacation, I make sure that I have a project that is set up to cover my vacation expenses. If a trip to Europe, Greece, or Africa is going to cost me $15,000, I must set up a deal that is going to make me at least $15,000 during that time. I have now bought the time that I want to spend traveling. Try thinking the same way.

Maybe you want to go on a vacation once a year, how much will it cost? If a deal doesn't earn enough to get you there, then don't take that deal. Also, think about how much money your time is worth. When I first started, I was involved in demo and clean-up at all my projects. By doing that, I was able to save a few thousand dollars, which originally was a game changer. Not so much now; it isn't worth me saving a few thousand on a deal by cleaning and knocking walls down for a few hours. I could've landed a deal worth a million instead.

Skill/Knowledge

The third criteria is your skill. This gets kind of tricky because you must honestly evaluate yourself and then decide where and what needs improvement for success in your real estate journey. HGTV always has shows like Power Couple or Fixer Upper; these couples or individuals travel the world, fixing people's houses. Now if you pay attention, some of these show hosts are super skilled. They set up walls and build custom bed frames and all this awesome stuff. Others seem to have a great idea, but when it comes to the actual work, they pass it on to their team. Here's my question: Which is better? Both! I personally don't have the best building skills, but I can see what needs to be done in a property. I tend to create the plan and then find someone with the skill to do the job well. It doesn't make sense for me to spend years of time and money, the first two criteria, learning these things. When you are looking at skill, you must find the balance between costs and profits, including your personal time as a cost.

Build Your Criteria

Things to consider:

1. What am I already skilled in;
2. What do I need to learn to be successful; and
3. Is it worth learning this, or will it cost me more time and money?

Talking with people and building connections is my natural skill set, a huge part of the real estate industry. Making the transition into the real estate world, I needed knowledge about how real estate worked. I looked for it. I attended my first masterclass in Atlanta. Since then, I have attended numerous other classes as well as discussed real estate with my partners, mentors, and others. The return on learning has been well worth the time and dime that it cost me.

You need to consider what skills you have and what you need to learn. Maybe you have building skills but need to understand more about the real estate industry. Maybe you already understand the industry but need to understand more about connecting and sharing your vision with people. Whatever your skill needs are, you must honestly realize the skills you have and the skills you need to learn to be successful in the real estate industry.

Dream Team

The fourth criteria involves building a dream team. Having evaluated yourself, you may notice that there are areas you need to find other people to fill. You may need a contractor, lawyer, or salesperson. My first deal in Atlanta was a complete failure. A wholesaler approached me about a house that was selling for $27,000. I happened to meet the owner directly, and he told me that he only wanted $16,000 for the property. It sounded like a deal, but I wanted to make sure that I didn't cut the wholesaler out. He reassured me. By the way, you pay the wholesaler if he closes the deal. We agreed to terms. I sent him the money, and he sent me the title. Sounded like a good deal, right? What was my mistake? Well, I didn't do my due diligence. The house had a tax lien on it for $11,000. This means that whatever I did with that house, I had to add an extra $11,000 to the cost. My mistake not having the right team in place. If I had established a good attorney on my team, the lien on the property would have been caught instantly. After I found out about the $11,000 lien, I immediately called a lawyer. A lawyer would've let me know that I didn't owe this guy anything. In the end, I spent an extra $22,000, $11,000 to the tax lien I hadn't known about and $11,000 to the wholesaler whom I could have saved the extra expense. In conclusion, I ended up selling the property for a loss. Lesson learned.

Location

The last criteria to build is location. If you have watched any business or real estate courses, you have probably heard the importance of *location, location, location.* As much as it is over talked about, we must talk about it. First, location is everything. A crappy house in a great location may do better than a great house in a crappy location. The key is understanding what makes a good location.

As you become an expert in this field, there may be hundreds of items on your checklist for what makes the best investment opportunity. For now, let's keep it simple. Honestly, the "perfect" investment does not exist. There will be challenges, losses, and many projects will require more work than you originally anticipated! Hang on because the reward will come. Don't seek perfection; seek possibility! Start with the centuries-old selling point: location, location, location. Where your potential investment property is located obviously matters! Before pinpointing a location, you must first understand your goal.

If your goal is obtaining a property that can be successfully rented and booked by tourists, you will have a higher chance of success when the location:

- Is in a widely popular city;
- Has access to great amenities;
- Is near shopping and entertainment;
- Is near famous landmarks; and
- Is close to beaches or other sources of outdoor recreation.

If your goal is owning and flipping a home, your success will mostly likely be dependent on locations:

- With access to good schools;
- In prime or growing neighborhoods;
- With low crime rates;
- With nearby amenities, shopping, and entertainment;
- If in a city, has a good walk score; and
- Surrounded by well maintained and groomed homes and businesses

Build Your Criteria

If you are seeking to stand out or bring value to neighborhoods that are not flourishing, then you will want to keep your eye out on properties that:

- Are in isolated, rural areas;
- Sections of major cities that are on the decline; and
- Are in barely recognized towns or cities.

If you are planning to immediately or eventually become a long-term landlord, your ideal locations will include:

- Markets with mostly mid to high-rent averages;
- Areas that are flourishing enough to encourage long-term renting;
- Access to nearby amenities, shopping, and entertainment; and
- If in the city, areas with a good walk score.

If you are planning on joining other investors to buy a property with combined capital, you will benefit from locations that:

- Are flourishing enough to catch multiple investors' eyes;
- In an area with a mid to high household earnings average; and

- Have access to nearby amenities, shopping, and entertainment.

Search! Search multiple opportunity options. You'll want to weigh the pros and cons of each type of building or property and evaluate your own level of personal interest to help decide which type of investment will be right for you. I began my journey specializing in single-family homes. That was part of my criteria, and I saw success from it. You may prefer multi-family or maybe commercial properties. The same principles apply.

Tour Your Neighborhood

Here is a fun homework assignment for you! Travel more. Near and far. Spend some time driving around prime areas and tour available properties. It is no surprise that there is nothing better than in-person, first-hand experience. Take pictures, walk around, ask for tours, and chat with neighbors and tenants and other owners as you search for the best opportunity. The more you expose yourself to various areas and properties, the better you can determine flourishing neighborhoods, community trends, and even understand local business trends. Start with your state and understand the various geographic areas. Then check out neighboring states and travel the nation. While traveling, you will begin to understand different markets and how different people think, allowing you to make more informed decisions when choosing your location.

When I started flipping houses, I decided to focus on Atlanta and the immediate suburb areas partly because I live in the area, and I love the area. The other part of my reason was strategy. For me, these areas checks all the boxes. The neighborhoods around Atlanta have access to shopping and attractions, a large city, and main roads. It makes real estate easy. For example, my Airbnbs are consistently filled with people coming for hospitals, theme parks, business meetings, and sports events. My long-term rentals and flips are filled with people who work for those same businesses. Whether you are considering a big market like NYC or Atlanta or considering a smaller suburb, location is crucial to your success.

Putting It All Together

Your criteria all work together to protect you and your investment and keep you focused on your real estate journey. Because each is dependent of each other, it's important to work through all your criteria before you start. For example, if you determine that you will handle much of your renovations by yourself, you lower your need for capital to pay a skilled laborer, but that only works if you have the time to invest into a project that won't pay you for a few months. Before you move on to the next chapter, I would highly recommend you sort out your criteria. In fact, I even left some space for you to do exactly that!

Notes: My Five Criteria

1. Capital:

2. Time:

3. Skill:

4. People:

Build Your Criteria

5. Location:

CHAPTER 5

Building Your Dream Team

I had landed an amazing opportunity to flip a house in Decatur, just outside of Atlanta. We had purchased the house in cash and were looking for a quick flip. I paid my contractor, and he promised he would get the job done. I had done some work with him before, so I took him at his word. I found out later that he didn't work on my house but turned it into a trap house. Let me be clear. A place where illegal drugs are sold is a trap house! I found out while showing the house to potential buyers. Imagine for a moment, showing up to a house and seeing drugs and people hanging around. Needless, to say, it was a hard situation to explain.

My contractor had gotten arrested for a DUI and couldn't finish my project. In addition to his arrest, he had the police to tow his car to my house, the one that he was supposed to be working on for me—my project house that he had turned into a trap house. So now I have an incomplete house, an unwanted car, changed locks, and a buyer who wants to close on the house. I did finish the project and sold it for $120,000. I still made profit of about $13,000, far less than it should've been. It's hard to ask for much money on a house when you must explain that the drug dealer in your house works for you.

Therefore, it is important to build a strong team while preparing to launch your real estate journey. Avoiding deals with contractors wanting to sell drugs out of your house happens through networking. Most of my partners I met at real estate investing events, through mutual friends, or at a party of some kind. Yes, I am working even when I'm having fun. When it comes to building a team, there are five people (or groups of people) you must get right.

Money Lenders

Unless you have access to an endless amount of money, you will have to borrow money throughout your real estate journey. The more properties and cash flow you want, the more money you will have to borrow. That's the reason it is important to build a strong relationship with investors and money lenders.

There are two main groups of money lenders: financial institutions or hard money lenders. Financial institutions like credit unions, mortgage brokers, or banks are probably the most well-known way to get money for your real estate deals. With few exceptions, their criteria for a house is pretty cut and dry. If you meet their criteria, they will give you a loan or mortgage based on your income, debt-to-income ratio, and the amount of money you are able to bring to the table. A traditional mortgage or loan is great for a long-term purchase like a rental but not the best for flipping houses.

Criteria for securing a typical mortgage from a financial institution:

1. Two years of tax returns, access to bank records, pay stubs, credit, and other identifying documents;
2. Proof of your debt-to-income ratio;
3. A down payment (typically 20 percent on a commercial deal);
4. Pay for an appraisal to be approved;
5. Property usually must be in "livable" condition; and
6. Thirty to forty-five days to close on the loan.

Another option from financial institutions is something that I use regularly—a line of credit. If you have a business, you can ask your bank to set you up with a line of credit. Often, they are willing to extend a certain amount to you based on your business income. If you don't have a business history of more than two years, they will still approve you for a line of credit, but you will be the guarantor.

Hard money lenders can be anyone who has access to cash and is willing to invest it with you. Many people invest with their friends and family. Jeff Bezos did this. On his way to building Amazon into a billion-dollar company, his parents were among the first to invest in him. Second, you can branch your circle of investors to complete "strangers." I say this because many times, investors can be people you barely know. With many of my deals, I connected with an investor who I had met through a friend. Although hard money loans typically carry a higher interest rate, the benefits of a hard money lender far outweigh the benefits of a bank loan:

1. You can have access to capital in a matter of days;
2. They are less concerned with credit score or tax returns;
3. They don't mind lending on "unlivable" properties; and
4. Typically have a shorter loan term.

Another bonus of hard money lenders is an added advisor to your business. Because banks want to make money from interest, they could care less on whether you are getting a good deal on your house. A hard money lender, however, makes their money from profit share or interest. Profit share means that you agree to split the profit from the house when you sell it. This usually looks like a 50/50 deal of some kind. The second way is interest as well. But they know that the chance of them not making their money goes up if it is a bad deal. Because of this, they are a bit more vested in you getting a good deal on the property. If you send your estimated project costs to them, and they decline, they probably have a good reason. Maybe they don't trust you, but most likely, they don't think it's a good deal. You may think you have a property that can sell for $250,000, but they think it will only sell for $180,000 and turn you down.

This is not always a bad thing. Yes, sometimes you need to go find another lender, but you might also need to take another look at your plans. Maybe the house won't hold the value that you think it should. Either way, it is your decision in the end, but always take a rejection from a lender with a grain of salt.

How to Get Private Lenders
Before asking for money, build your pitch. Remember, you are talking to people that may or may not know you, yet you are

convincing them to lend you money. To do this successfully, you must answer two questions.

Why should I trust you?
For me, the answer goes like this: "I've purchased and renovated over 8.5 million dollars of real estate in the last six years. You can check out my website and view my portfolio."

What will you do for me?
For me: "I can get you 20 percent on your money through real estate. This is a much better investment than a savings account in the bank. It's comparable to the stock market and a very safe, proven investment."

The key is to keep your response as concise and clear as possible. Yes, you can explain more about your business and success if they ask, but you want to keep it to the point. The other important key is to be confident. Whether it is your first flip or your hundredth, be confident. Find ways (without lying) to promote confidence in your vision. Remember, people invest in people, not ideas. Yes, you want to show your knowledge of the real estate deal and showcase your track record, but at the end of the day, be personable. Show that you are a likeable, trustworthy person.

Eventually, you will have a network of lenders built, and you will be able to tap into that network whenever you need to access additional capital. At the beginning of your real estate journey, take what you can get and build a track record. The more often you get someone's money back to them with a profit, the more often they will give you money. They may even recommend you to their investor friends.

Deal-Finder

Once you have established a network of investors to fund your first deal, well, you need to find a deal. In the early days, I was very involved in finding my own deals. I would drive through Atlanta looking for houses, connecting with house buyers and sellers at events, and pretty much devoting most of my time to finding a deal. I've always been pretty good at finding deals, and I enjoy it. However, nowadays, I do work with a network of wholesalers and other investors to find my deals. I still enjoy it, but allowing others to do some of the preliminary legwork gives me more time to focus on other areas of my business. If you don't have time to find deals, there are people who can help.

Wholesaler/Bird-Dogger

For a fee, usually a small percentage of the final purchase price, a wholesaler will connect you with property owners who have not yet listed their properties on the market. The seller is either not actively looking to sell, or there is an obstacle preventing them. Examples of obstacles: a distressed property, no capital to repair the building, personal problems, or just wanting to sell the property quickly. Whatever the motive is or the obstacle, a wholesaler is a great connection for finding off-market properties that are a great deal.

Real Estate Agent

A real estate agent can also be a great person to work with. The key is finding someone who is "investor friendly." These are the same as a regular agent, but they understand that you are looking for a good deal, not a dream house. Investor friendly real estate agents will shift their focus to finding houses that need work and match your investing criteria. These agents are willing to work with you because they still receive a commission from the sale.

How to Find a Deal-Finder

You may be wondering how to find a deal-finder. The answer is simple. Whether you are looking for a wholesaler or a real estate agent, the answer is the same: networking. You can meet potential real estate agents at real estate networking events like the REIA. REIA stands for Real Estate Investing Association, and they're nationwide. Do you want a wholesaler? Just Google, *real estate clubs near me*. I met my first wholesaling partner at a networking event, and although my first deal was a bust, it did get me in the game. I was able to quickly strike one bad business partner off the list. Once you have a list of potential partners, continue your research. Try to find out what it is like to work with them. Ask to meet with them and just get a feel for them. Ask for a list of referrals from previous clients.

Once you have narrowed down your list, it's time to reach out. You can call or send an email. Whichever you choose to do, you should send the following message:

> "Hello, my name is_____. I'm a real estate investor in (city), and I'm looking for discounted properties in the area. If you're willing to bring me many offers, please give me a call at your earliest convenience."

If they contact you, that's a good sign that they are a good candidate for your team. Finding the right deal is the most time-consuming part of investing. Even with your criteria set in place, the hardest part of finding the right deal is making sure it's the right one. You may make dozens of offers before you land your first deal. That's okay. Real estate is a numbers game. The more offers that are turned down means you are closer to closing on a deal. Another reason for building a good team of deal-finders is that after a while, some may quit. Finding deals can be much work, and some may not be willing.

Contractors

As I said earlier, I helped with demo and cleaning early in my career, but I certainly was not a professional in construction. Although I have picked up tips and knowledge over the years, I certainly wouldn't consider myself an expert. The good thing is that you don't need to ever fully understand construction nor be able to do construction. You are a real estate investor, not a tradesman. Unless you become really good with tools and enjoy the process, you shouldn't be involved in this process. No matter how good you are, you can only fix so many houses at one time. You need to make sure you have a good team in place to help you with your home renovations. Finding the right contractor can be difficult. You will need to make a checklist. Include these items on the checklist for finding contractors:

1. **Licensed:** The first step is make sure they are licensed. No matter how good they are, your house will not see if you hire a contractor with no license. In fact, any work that is without a license will most likely have to be undone and redone properly. Asking for a license is simple. If proof of license is refused, they probably don't have one.

2. **Contractor Shopping:** Contractors are a bit harder to find than a good real estate agent or even a wholesaler. Good ones are hard to come by, so people aren't as willing to share them. The best place to get a head start on finding contractors is posting on Craigslist, searching Google, or visiting your local hardware store. You can talk to the staff at the help desk at any hardware store and let them know you are looking for a contractor. When you do find a good contractor, just like a property, make sure you vet them. Ask for a physical walkthrough of one of their projects, and ask for client referrals. A bad contractor can turn a great deal into a horrible one by slowing your project or racking up additional expenses.

3. **Contracts:** Once you have found good contractor, it's time for a contract. Before they start working, work out the cost, payment schedule, and other details of a project. Yes, you will want to get started immediately, but don't do anything until you have something in writing. The written contract will protect you and the contractor in case of any unforeseen issues or disagreements.

You will want to follow the same process for your appraiser and your inspector.

Appraisers — assess the value of your house. This is very important when you are looking to purchase a house. You want to get a good idea of what the house may be worth after renovating it. If you have a typo or bad appraisal, it could cost thousands of dollars. Appraisers, just like contractors, are paid per house appraised. Your bank will provide an official appraiser, but it's good to also have one on your team or at least someone you can access.

Inspectors — will identify all structural or safety issues in the home. They are less concerned with price value than they are with the safety. Inspectors will let you know if the house needs upgrades to be compliant with code or if the house has foundation damage or other damages. House inspectors are also paid per house they inspect.

Legal Team
Often, passive investors or group investors don't hire an attorney to help ensure legal contracts and smooth closings because someone else involved in the project typically brings in a lawyer of their choosing to help the venture close. However, a second- or third-party attorney does not specifically represent

your best interest. If you are working with a real estate agent, your contract with them often includes a lawyer to represent you at closing. But if you are working with investors and opting to exclude an agent, you should absolutely consult an attorney. Investing in real estate will be one of your largest investments. Protect your venture, from start to finish, by having someone who thoroughly understands real estate and corporate laws to evaluate your deal and represent your best interests.

Escrow Agent

You may have heard of an escrow agent. They operate similarly to a lawyer but with a focus only on the title. When you sign a contract, the escrow agent researches the title, making sure there is no fraudulent activity attached to the title, and they will also offer title insurance, helping protect you if any issues arise even after you close.

Accounting Team

The next person you need on your team is a good accountant. An accountant is a financial professional who handles the bookkeeping and prepares financial documents: profit-and-loss statements, balance sheets, and so forth. Accountants perform audits of your books, prepare reports for tax purposes, and handle all the financial information that's part of running your business. This is especially important for real estate, with the costs and large amounts of money moving, and making sure all finances are in order.

Conclusion

Your team is the key to your success. Each member of your team will play a specific role in helping you build your real estate empire. You may not need a large team at the beginning of your journey, but you will definitely need to make sure they are the right fit. When I started, I was only linked with one hard money lender, a friend of mine, and one wholesaler. I quickly learned that I needed to build that team so that I could keep deals coming. Now I literally work with hundreds of people making my deals work, contractors, lawyers, and investors, I stay pretty busy. My team is the reason that I have the success that I have. Before getting your big team, find the initial team. Maximize what you can do with your initial team and then look to build a bigger team!

Notes:
List Potential Members for Your Dream Team

1. Lender

2. Deal-Finder

3. Contractor/Managers:

Inspector:

_____

_____

_____

_____

_____

_____

_____

Licensed Contractor:

_____

_____

_____

_____

_____

_____

_____

4. Legal Team

5. Accountant

Qualifying Questions to Ask:

- Do you work with real estate investors? How are your fees paid?
- When are your fees due?
- What are your areas of expertise?

CHAPTER 6

THE ART OF THE DEAL

Finding a deal is the lifeblood of real estate. Once you have your dream team in place, find a good deal. The first step in finding a good deal is understanding the expenses that go into a real estate purchase. You've probably realized that a house costs more than just the price listed. A basic formula for buying a house would look something like this.

Sale Price – Purchase Price – Renovation Cost – Realtor Fees = Profit

This would be a great formula—if it were true. The problem is that there are many "hidden fees" within a real estate deal. The biggest fee for an investor is the holding cost. This is the price it costs to hold a property until you have sold it. This includes any interest and payments you are making to your lender, any utilities payments, and any other expenses associated with holding a property. You also must include closing costs, which pay for your attorney, a title company, if using one, and other fees associated with finalizing the deal. That still isn't including what I call "dumb" fees or miscellaneous fees. Just like it sounds, this should always be factored in for when you have to tow a car after your contractor is arrested, paying for lost keys, or any other "dumb" things. No matter how well you prepare and track, there are always unexpected expenses. When you include these additional costs, your formula will look more like this.

Sales Price – Purchase Price – Renovation Costs – Realtor Fees – Holding Costs – Closing Costs – Dumb Fees = Profit

Sale Price
How much money a home is selling for

Purchase Price
How much money you pay for the home

Renovation Costs
The total cost of all the repairs of a home to get the after-repair value you're looking for

Realtor Fees
How much you paid out to the realtors

Holding Costs
The cost of the property taxes, insurance, and utilities while you hold a property.

Money Costs
How much you paid your lenders for the money.

Closing Costs
All the fees and transfer tax paid to title company and lawyers

Dumb Fees
Any fees that weren't planned on for the project. Replacing lost keys, paying for damaged property, and so on.

When I first started in real estate, I didn't know about these additional costs. I've always been a money planner, planning each project—down to the penny—and didn't allow for additional costs. Needless to say, a few deals into my journey, I realized that there were many extra expenses. This is probably the costliest mistake for new investors. Not accounting for the extra expenses, you may break even or lose money on your deals. As you evaluate deals, you will want to keep all these different costs in mind. Whatever money is left over after paying all these costs is your profit.

Evaluating Costs

If miscalculating the additional costs that go into a real estate deal is the greatest mistake, then underestimating repair costs is probably the second. While it may not seem like a big deal to be off a few thousand dollars on an estimate, every dollar you add into expenses cuts into your profit. You must be familiar with the saying, "Don't judge a book by its cover." This is no longer just a catchy phrase; this is your principle to live by. I want you to always know that structure is greater than beauty. Sure, a beautiful, polished property is ideal, but don't count out cosmetic fixer-ups! As you grow in this industry, you will learn that even a house that is about to fall apart but located in a prime area, on a prime lot, is a goldmine! For now, baby steps. Set your eyes on solid structures with great potential.

The table below includes an average price for common repairs as of 2022.

Cost of Repairs

When you are viewing a property, you want to make sure the structure of the building is good. If not, be careful. These repairs are much more expensive than cosmetic repairs.

Structural repairs include:

- Plumbing;
- Framing;
- Electricity;
- Flooring; and
- Home expansion.

If any of these components require repair, be careful! This can get expensive fast and may kill an otherwise attractive deal. The biggest component is understanding your budget and resources. Cosmetic changes and finishes are often easy to fix and, in many cases, affordable. Cosmetic repairs consist of repairing the following items:

- Light fixtures;
- Paint;
- Décor;
- Shelving;
- Appliances;
- Doors;
- Cabinets;
- Kitchen or bathroom upgrades; and
- Other finishes.

One thing I want to point out is the difference between small upgrades and complete renovations. Gutting a bathroom is an expensive and time-consuming endeavor that includes new plumbing, new electric, fixtures, flooring, and tearing down and building a wall. This can get quite expensive. However, simply upgrading a vanity or tub can make a world of difference without breaking the bank. Below is a chart that compares prices for structural changes and cosmetic changes—notice the price difference.

Structural Change	Average National Price	Cosmetic Changes	Avg. Price
Plumbing	Repipe: $8,200 New Installation: $5,000–$15,000	New Vanity and Tub	$800–$5,000
Electric wiring	$2,000–9,000 depending on square footage	Light Fixtures	$200
Brick a home	$9–$26 per square foot	Paint	$3–$4 per sq. ft $2,500–$3,600 (exterior total)
Install siding	$5,000–$16,000		" "
Installing carpet	$3–$6 per square foot		" "
Installing hardwood floors	$10–$23 per square foot	Shelving	$14–$23 per linear square foot
Bathroom gut and remodel	$10,000–$15,000 for smaller bathrooms; $50,000+ for large bathrooms	New counters	$2,000–$4,000
Kitchen gut and remodel	$13,000–$35,000	New Cabinets & Appliances	$2,500–$30,000
Home expansion	$86–$208 per square feet	New doors	$1,500–$3,000 $730 interior door

Making a Profit

There are multiple different formulas calculating a good deal, but it comes down to this simple concept: You need to make more money than you spend. You will accomplish this by understanding your cost and selling price. One formula you may want to consider using is determining your minimum profit. This is the easiest formula to calculate. When you look at a project, ask yourself, *What is the minimum profit I want to make on this house?* Obviously, this will vary from project to project, but it's helpful to set some guidelines. My guidelines are super simple.

1. Minimum profit should be 20 percent or more of the ARV.
2. Minimum profit should be $60,000.

The first rule keeps me from getting burned on my larger deals. A $25,000 profit may sound like an awesome deal, but that is not always the case. Imagine, selling a house for $1,000,000 and only making $25,000. Yes, it's a profit, but it's not worth the time and money for a 2-percent return! It also protects you from making an unnecessary risk. If your profit margin on a $1,000,000 house is only $20,000, then you will most likely end up losing money. What if the best offer is for $950,000? You have now lost $30,000. If you follow the 20-percent rule, which is a conservative number, you still make money.

The second rule keeps me from spending money on deals that aren't worth my time. If I follow the 20-percent rule, I may find myself with properties that meet those criteria but really end up being a waste of my time. A house that has an ARV of $100,000 will make me $20,000. That's good but not worth the time and risk. Having a benchmark of $60,000 keeps my attention on larger deals that will push me closer to my goals faster and are a better use of my time. Another factor of working with deals that are so low is that you run into the same issue as with the $1,000,000 home. If you are anticipating a $20,000 profit but run into an unexpected repair, you can eat up your profit very quickly.

ARV (After Repair Value)

This is the most important number in a real estate deal. No matter how cheaply you buy a property and how tight you are on your renovation budget, this is the number that determines if you make a profit or not. This number is not always the easiest to compute. The best way to calculate a home's ARV is by comparison to comparable properties. These properties include active listings in your neighborhood, recently sold properties, and other factors. Other factors would include your house-specific items like the square footage of the house. This can decrease or increase the value of the house accordingly. What is the price of other renovated homes in the area?

Timing

Generally, in real estate, speed is the way to get good deals and make more money. Remember the house that my contractor turned into a trap house? Part of the reason that house ended up being a bust was the time it took to complete the renovations. When I came back from my cruise, it turns out he hadn't done any work. I came to the house and was surprised to see pipes, wood, and other construction materials lying around the inside and outside of the house. As much as that hurt, the holding costs and the cost of hiring another contractor were what hurt me most. I ended up having to hold that property for seven months when it should've been sold in just a few months. In all, I ended up paying an additional $40,000 on the property. I still managed to get a $20,000 profit on the house, yet it should've been well above that. As well as outlandish contractors, there are a few other time factors that will affect your deal.

Slow Economy

When the economy is doing well, real estate investors have a better chance of doing well. However, in times like 2019, when we were hit unexpectedly with a global pandemic, the economy played a wild card that is still being monitored. Investors everywhere are looking to see if the marketplace is too risky an investment. Interest rates are great indicators for economic investments like stocks, bonds, and real estate. Lower interest rates can indicate lower mortgages and be optimal for refinancing. A slow economy also affects production, labor, and supply costs. There have been shortages of homes and supplies, increasing competition. When the former recession transpired, shortages became the major issue. In our current economy, it is vital for investors to be prepared for the interruption of home demands. During unprecedented times, the rate of properties will not likely decrease. Making vital investments that will sustain your profit is still possible in a slow economy but much more challenging.

Buyer's Market[1]

A great investor pays keen attention to the cycle of the market. One of the most fundamental ways to look at the real estate market is by assessing whether it is a buyer's market or seller's market. A buyer's market means that owners are not selling property as quickly as usual. This often means that owners are more malleable with the terms of the contract and even the price of the property. The seller's market is when real estate properties are highly sought after. The demand for people who want to buy has increased.

During a seller's market, buyers may even pay above the asking price because they want the property. Paying close attention to the market can be the difference in buying an expensive property that will yield a great return or buying an expensive property that will plummet in profit because of the market change.

---

[1] *https://www.dummies.com/personal-finance/investing/mastering-sellers-buyers-markets-invest-real-estate/*

Following the foundations of real estate is vital for knowing if you will buy or sell property and, most of all, if you will gain profit.

Global or National Crisis

A global crisis such as the 2020–2021 pandemic has been one of the most unpredictable moments in history. The markets quickly took a hit like the recession in 2008. Due to a decrease in foreign travel and affairs, many investors saw a decrease in purchases from foreign buyers. Second, during such a complex time, many are losing jobs, unable to keep up with living expenses, which can also put landlords in a position of debt if the property remains vacant or unpaid. Consequently, this can leave owners in positions of foreclosure. However, there may be a positive shift that results from such a time in that those who have invested in stocks may pull out their money and invest it in real estate. This could possibly cancel out the decline and demand of property value. During crises, as an investor, you must be mindful of possible debt and vacancies. If you will still make a profit after all conditions have been weighed, you may be in a position of return despite an unpredictable time.

Lack of Cash Flow[2]

Cash flow is the primary vehicle to accessing prime investment opportunities and gaining profit. It is a simple concept: Cash flow must outweigh the expense of the property. If not, this will leave your cash flow in the negative. You will then have to pay out of pocket to cover the expenses. It is common that some investors may have this experience from time to time. If the property is a great investment, it may flourish despite an unpredictable time. However, constant negative cash flow can leave the investor in a deficit and curtail potential deals.

Outlandish Vendors and Contractors[3]

One of the most complex relationships is between the owner of the property and the contractor. We were building a house for a celebrity in Atlanta. He wanted a custom-made staircase that required an iron welder to complete. We had a hold on the inspection because the welder messed up the steps—even after coming back three times to fix it. Finally, we ended up getting another welder to finish the job because we couldn't contact the original guy. Once the staircase had been completed, the original welder appeared at the home. He had been arrested. We told him the job was done. The original welder entered the

---

[2] *https://learn.roofstock.com/blog/what-every-real-estate-investor-needs-to-know-about-cash-flow*

[3] *https://www.lendinghome.com/blog/how-to-deal-with-a-bad-contractor/*

house to get his tools. It seemed like all was well until a few days later when we got a call from our celebrity client. Apparently, the original welder let his brother take a tour and pictures of the whole house, which he posted on social media, tagging the celebrity. Our client was pretty upset, and we fought to keep that contract.

Contractors are always tricky. The owner needs the contractor for repairs and renovations, no matter how big or small the job. However, the relationship can get testy and irritable, especially when large amounts of money are involved. Also, doing crazy things like selling drugs out of your house, posting random tours, shooting and messing around a celebrity's home, and other issues always occur. Some major issues occur when a contractor's work is not efficient, yet the contractor may still want to be paid for the job. The contractor going over budget is another issue that can come up during property renovation. The expenses for contracting are costly and can drain your pockets if not closely monitored and managed. Preventing many of the complications caused by inadequate contractors, be sure to screen the company and contact previous jobs to evaluate their work. Get several quotes from credible contractors. Finally, clearly know your property needs, allow the contractor to finish a smaller job, then decide if the contractor is a match for your needs.

Wrong Business Partner[4]

Remember the deal that I ended up getting completely boxed out of because I didn't do my due diligence? Besides the obvious fact that I was naïve to start working without a contract, there is another lesson in that story. Choose your business partners wisely. A business partner can be of great benefit when going into investment. Having another individual who is financially stable can provide strong capital and help cover costs. A partner who has experienced the process of real estate investing can be a great asset. Ideally, they have knowledge and skills that are not yours. Maybe they have quick access to capital. When you find a deal, your business partners are able to move quickly to fund it, allowing you to move faster throughout the buying and selling process.

In any relationship, there can be complications. To prevent or even navigate the business relationship, create a contract or agreement of sort that holds each partner accountable. Terms should clearly explain actionable precautions that can be made if terms are broken. Lastly, it is not required, but having a legal advisor or lawyer could be beneficial in the event of any mishaps in a business partnership. If legalities, common respect, and equal work ethics are not shared, then

---

[4] *https://realestate.usnews.com/real-estate/articles/the-pros-and-cons-of-investing-in-real-estate-with-a-partner*

not only the real estate deal but also your reputation may be harmed, ruining your entire investment, and slowing down operations.

There are multiple reasons a partner can be a bad fit. They move too slow, are dishonest, or have different goals. Whatever the reason, try to avoid bad partners and keep good ones.

Bad Location[5]

Location! Location! Location! Making solid investment choices requires more research and understanding of the property's location beyond its address or neighborhood. There are a few factors that determine whether a location is considered prime or risky. Throughout this industry, you will hear the phrase "triple A." The "triple A" stands for amenities, accessibility, and appearance. This is a standard way of rating a property in a neighborhood. A location that has minimal access to commuting like highways or transportation is a problem for people who travel for work. Does the location have community amenities, such as parks, recreation, and nature, and grocery stores or shopping centers? Often, buyers are not interested in a location that has little to no development for the future for these amenities: schools, hospitals,

---

[5] *https://www.investopedia.com/financial-edge/0410/the-5-factors-of-a-good-location.aspx*

or commercial infrastructure since such developments may increase property values. The fewer "triple A" ratings a property has, the harder the property will be to sell. A few times in my career have I gotten stuck with a bad location, which led to a headache and loss of money.

Unrealistic Expectations

One of the most common reasons that a real estate deal fails or an investor is unpleased with the results is unrealistic expectations. This industry really attracts people who want the unattainable! Please hear my words—you must do the work, and you must have patience. Real estate will never be a get-rich-quick scheme. There will be times in your career when amazing deals are presented to you that sound incredibly prosperous. Some deals have no hiccups and yield substantial results. These are real estate unicorns—deals with no hiccups and a large return. Most of the time as a real estate investor, you simply must wait it out. Most importantly, you can only get the level of ROI that matches your investment.

I host lawn chair learning circles throughout Atlanta, where I meet with new investors yearning to grow their investment portfolios. I answer investment questions and offer insight into this ever-changing business. I am still shocked at how many new investors invest $2,000–$10,000 into a real estate deal and are terribly disappointed when their deal doesn't yield six figures in ninety days! It is essential to view real estate investing as a full-time business. You can't get something for nothing. The more money you invest, the more time you yield or at least someone on your team.

Notes: This Was a Tricky Chapter, So Let's Go Over Some of the Key Points.

1. Cost Formula

2. Definition of ARV

3. Your ARV Goal

4. Eight Time Factors

CHAPTER 7

MAKING OFFERS

Until now, we have discussed the basics of real estate and understanding the costs that go into finding a good deal. Now we will discuss how to make an offer on a property.

Be Willing to Make Low Offers

Once you connect with the right opportunity, it's important to start with the end in mind. The best investors in real estate are willing to walk away from a deal that doesn't have the right price. If the price is not right, there are plenty of other deals; walk away and find the next one. If a house is listed for $200,000, but you think it's only worth $140,000, offer $130,000 and see what happens. If the answer is no, increase your price so it seems like you are willing to negotiate but never come right in at the highest price you are willing to pay. The best deals may come when you are the solution to a distressed seller.

Makes Many Offers

Many of your offers will not get accepted. That means you will need to make a lot more offers before making a deal. If a property meets your criteria, and you have your team in place, make an offer. Your chance at success goes up the more offers you make. It's a numbers game.

You Can Make Remote Offers

At the beginning of my career, I tried to personally view every property I wanted to make an offer on. At first, this was good. I needed to learn and physically see things. Once my skills were honed, this became impractical. You should be able to tell what a property needs through pictures. If your deal is accepted, then you personally view the property to verify. If it's different than the pictures, then you can renegotiate or cancel the deal altogether. This must be completed during your due diligence period.

Be Fast

Never rush, but you do need to be decisive and quick. Once you are certain you have a good deal, quickly make an offer. If you think it's a good deal, someone else may think it's a good deal too. In my real estate journey, there have been many deals that I missed by minutes.

Another way to save time on an offer is to make verbal or text offers before writing an official offer. Writing an official offer takes too much time—especially if you are considering multiple offers a day. You should only write up an official offer when you are ready to close a deal.

When you are ready to close a deal, here are some basic elements that will be on your contract.

Purchase Price. How much you're paying for the house.

Close Date. What day the deal will be complete, generally phrased as "On or before"

Earnest Money Deposit (EMD). This is money that you give to the title company. It serves as a deposit to show that you are serious or earnest about purchasing the property. If you don't close on the property, you may lose this money.

Due Diligence Period. This is the time you need to contact your contractors and get your inspection in. A shorter period is riskier but shows the seller that you are more serious about your offer. However, if you can't get your inspections done in time, you risk losing your EMD.

Since, as an investor, I will most likely never have an offer with the highest purchase price, here are some ways that I use the other terms of the contract to make my offer more appealing.

How to Make an Attractive Offer

Close Date in One Week.
When you are working with cash and your own team, you can speed up the closing process. The typical deal closes in thirty to forty-five days, and you should offer a faster closing period. This shows the buyer that you can move quickly and get them their money quickly as well. This give you a huge advantage with sellers.

Larger EMD Than They Ask For
Putting down a larger EMD is a risk. If you don't close, you could lose all that money. AS long as you know you're going to buy the property, this shouldn't be an issue and will make your offer look more attractive. In this scenario, you haven't changed the purchase price, but you have shown the seller that you are a serious buyer.

Shorten the Due Diligence Period
The standard Due Diligence Period is seven to ten days. If you can short this to one to three days, you show them you

are willing to get your inspections in, your team is ready, and have contractor quotes in quickly, allowing you to get the deal done quickly. It also shows that you are confident in the deal, because if you don't get your Due Diligence done, you risk losing your EMD. This is risky but well worth it if you can move with that speed.

Loan Contingency

I didn't include this in the previous list, but this is a bonus of working with cash lenders. Most contracts have a loan contingency. Your offer is only valid if you can secure a loan. When you are working with your own cash and cash from investors, you don't have to worry about that contingency. Leaving this out of a contract shows that you can move on a deal quickly.

Pay All the Closing Costs

Offer to pay all closing costs when you are dealing directly with a seller. Yes, this takes an additional 3 percent out of your profit, but it also allows you to leverage to a lower price. The seller will be more willing to lower the price if they know they don't have to cover closing costs.

Warning: These are more advanced strategies for negotiating. Don't attempt this until you are confident you are able to deliver every time.

Once you have an accepted offer, you now need to step into action and fast.

1. **EMD.** Typically, you have twenty-four to forty-eight hours to deposit your EMD.

2. **Get your inspections and contractor bids.** Due Diligence Period starts as soon as your offer is accepted; you need to contact your inspections and bids before that period ends.

3. **Secure your loan.** Your money isn't due until the close date, but you need to move quickly. You will need to contact your lenders the same day the offer is accepted to start analyzing the deal.

4. **Final Walkthrough.** When your loan has been approved, make sure to walk through the property one more time before you send your money. Things happen, and you want to make sure that the property is still in the same condition as when you originally inspected it. If it's not, you either renegotiate or walk away from the door.

5. **Close the deal.** If the final walkthrough goes well and everything looks acceptable, wire the remaining money owed for the house. Now, your attorney or title company records the sale and processes all paperwork. Congratulations! You have just purchased a property.

Notes: Making Notes

1. How to Make An Attractive Offer

2. Steps after Getting an Accepted Offer

CHAPTER 8

Working with Contractors

Now that you have purchased the property, you still are only halfway through the process. You can't rest yet because now you need to renovate your house and sell it. This is probably one of the most frustrating aspects of real estate—dealing with contractors.

What Needs to Be Fixed?
You should already have a good idea of this before you purchase the house, but it is time to finalize your renovation plans for the house. There are no rules for the appearance of your house unless there's a strict HOA or you are in a historic community. You must study the neighboring properties to get an idea. Otherwise, if you needed any structural repairs done on the house, you need to do that first.

While structural repairs are done, decide on how to finish the house. All homes are slightly different depending on the market, price, and maybe even the layout. When I am renovating a $1,000,000 home, I use different materials and color schemes than I would on a $250,000 home. That is why it is important to study the market.

The best way is to copy what sells. Look at photos of at least three homes that sold quickly in the same area; study your successes as well. When you find something that seems to work, keep doing that. First, you guarantee that your house will sell faster, and it also allows you to finish more quickly when you don't have to make a decision on basic colors and styles for every single house.

Choose Your Contractor

Call your team. You should already have had several of your contractors look at the property during your due diligence phase. It is time to assign one of them to the project. You will want to choose from your list based on a few different things. First, choose based on time. Make sure you choose a contractor who can quickly finish the project. Remember, most contractors will go over the time they give, so keep that in mind. Second, of course, go with the best bid. This will include price but also quality of work. Keep in mind that a contractor is trying to get a job. This means they will tell you what they think you want to hear. Be careful not to believe everything they say at face value. I mostly work with very good contractors, but now and then, they stretch the truth to get a deal.

Pay Your People

Many contractors will ask you to pay a lot of money up front. Don't do that. Remember the guy who took my $30,000 and got arrested? While a contractor may not get arrested, they certainly can run into issues; some skip town, or sometimes they end up not being the man for the job. A rule of thumb is to stay ahead of your contractor. Ask yourself, if your contractor walked out today, would it cost more money to hire another contractor to finish the construction? If yes, they are ahead of me. If I am ahead, then they need to keep working so they don't lose out on the project.

At the beginning, they will be ahead of you. You will need to give them a down payment for supplies and hiring the additional people they need. After that initial payment, don't give them any more money until they have done good work. Always work out a payment plan with them but be willing to not pay them if they aren't getting the job done. The biggest mistake I made early on in my real estate journey was not following up on my contractors that cost me more money than I care to admit. Now, all my properties are checked on at least once or twice a week. Keep your contractors accountable. A pro tip is to take video and pictures every time you show up at the worksite. This keeps everyone honest if any disagreements arise. Not to mention, it can make good content for social media.

Additional Charges

While working through any project, you may often run into issues not in the original plan. This can be the biggest cause of conflict during a renovation, the result of finding issues that are not on the original bid: mold that needs cleaning or faulty wiring needing to be fixed (hidden before opening up a wall), and so on. There are many legitimate reasons that a job can cost more time and dime than originally thought, but you need to keep a hand on these changes. Don't let your contractor add anything to the bill without your approval first, via change order. It's pivotal to do this to everyone because you will forget some of the smaller changes that can add up in the end to thousands of dollars. Imagine having to explain cost over runs totaling thousands of dollars in hundred-dollar increments. And if they do, fight to pay it and never use them again. In a game of numbers, you need to make sure that you are in control of every dollar that you spend on a project.

Final Walkthrough

For the same reason that you want to do a final walkthrough before you close on a property, make a final walkthrough before making your final payment to a contractor. Once they tell you the job is complete, follow up. You want to check the quality of their work. Look for any paint spots that were missed. Make sure cabinets, drawers, and doors all open and close properly. Do your lights work? Do all showers, faucets, and toilets work? Are there any leaks? You'll want to check any seals on doors, windows, or where the wall meets the floor. Make sure there are no gaps or inconsistencies. Lastly, make sure the heating and air-conditioning system works. Once you have finished checking the quality of the work, then match their work against the bid. Is there anything that still needs to be repaired that wasn't on the bid? If yes, get a quote on fixing it.

Conclusion

There are good contractors and bad contractors. Your job as an investor is to find the good ones who do good work, are trustworthy, and fairly priced. Once you find them, keep them busy! You don't want to lose them to another employer. Good and fairly priced contractors are too hard to come by to lose them to someone else for no reason. If a contractor doesn't work out, fire them. Don't be afraid to do that. You will find that it will cost you more time and headaches if you keep trying to work with a bad contractor. Grounds for firing are simple: if they aren't doing good work, are way behind schedule, or are overcharging or stealing from you. If they are behind, or their work is bad, give them a week to fix the problem. If they still can't do it right, it's time to look for a new contractor. Be sure these terms are in your contract so you're not left holding the bag. However, if they are stealing, that's grounds for firing on the spot.

Notes:

1. How to Evaluate a Contractor's Bid (Time, Quality, Price)

2. List of Contractors to Work With

CHAPTER 9

MAKING MONEY

Finally, the chapter we have all been waiting for. Up until this point, it has been pretty much all about spending money and dealing with people. Now we are going to talk about the final step, how to sell your house for the highest profit possible.

Hire a Realtor

The biggest mistake I made in the beginning of my journey was trying to sell my own properties. I figured I could save myself a few thousand dollars and sell directly to my buyers. After not selling my house for a few months, I then realized it was costing me more trying to sell my house myself. That's when I started building connections with strong real estate agents. And I know some people will go to even greater lengths to get their license just to save money. If you are an agent and genuinely love it, then it is a great way to vertically integrate. If you're only doing it to save money, don't. It will cost you more in the long run not having a skilled agent who is in tune with the trends of a community and actively working with buyers to negotiate the best possible outcome. I try to be generous with my real estate agents. I typically offer 3.5 percent commission and sometimes 4 percent if I think they will have trouble selling a property. At the end of the day, you want your real estate agent motivated to make you the most money for your property.

Take Good Pictures

Hire a professional. If you have bad or less than professional pictures, you will end up costing yourself thousands of dollars on every house you sell. When it comes to real estate, people always purchase with their eyes first. A good photographer may charge you up $500, but it is worth it. You may be tempted to take pictures yourself or hire your cousin who does photography on the side. Don't. Let me repeat myself. Hire a professional.

Decide on Your Listing Price

There is a bit more strategy that goes into choosing a price than just how much money you want to make. As we discussed earlier, ARV is always a good starting point, but sometimes you may want to go higher. Often, I have made an extra dollar just by "over-listing" my property. Sometimes if you anticipate much activity on a property, it may be a good strategy to "underprice" your property and let the different offers drive the price sky high. Be careful. This strategy only works if you are sure the property will be hot. Consult with your team and mentors on the best price. At the end of the day, unless your strategy is to create a bidding war, start high. It's a lot easier to come down on a price than go up.

List Your Property

Now that you have chosen your price, it's time to put the property on the market. A good rule of thumb is to put your property on the market on a Thursday or Friday. It will pop up as a new listing for the weekend when most people are trying to view many homes. This is a good rule of thumb, but if you are ready to post on a Sunday or Monday, do it! No need to waste potential selling days because you are waiting for the perfect day to sell your property.

Receive Offers

Once you put your house on the market, you will start to receive offers. The best case is that you get multiple offers on a property, and you have options on which offer you want to accept. There are three basic strategies to choosing an offer.

Accept the Best Offer: Maybe you received an offer that is a cash deal, and they are ready to close in a matter of days. You would be silly to not accept that offer. Remember, every day on the market, your holding costs are going up.

Counter the Best Offer: Maybe the best offer is pretty good, but you don't like some of the terms. Look at your price, close date, due diligence length, and so on. If there is anything you don't like, counter with your preferred terms.

Request Highest and Best. Maybe you received many good offers, but you want to see how high you can go. Inform all your potential buyers that you received many offers, and you will choose the highest and best offer. Give them a day or two to change their offer. Choose the offer that makes the most sense for you.

All of these strategies are great ways to sell your house if you are receiving multiple good offers. Sometimes your listing doesn't go so quickly, and you need to re-evaluate your offer.

The typical property is on the market for about three to four weeks before you receive your first offer. You have less power here than if your property is getting many offers in its first few days, but you still need to be wise in choosing an offer. You may not get all the terms you want, but you need to make sure you are still making a profit. You will need to work with the potential buyer and compromise. Find a way to make a deal that is beneficial for everyone. This is the power of a strong realtor; they will negotiate on your behalf.

Accepting an Offer

When you accept an offer, the buyer will go through the same process that you went through when you originally purchased the property. They will have a period of due diligence that allows them to have an inspector and an appraiser go through the property. If anything comes up as an issue, you need to address it before you can close the deal. The biggest concern here is if the inspector finds something that needs a repair. If this happens, you will need to address fixing the problem before finishing the sale; either you lower your price, or you pay a contractor to correct the issue.

One issue that I ran into was with an appraisal. The property had been appraised at $250,000, but the buyer's appraiser only appraised it at $235,000. When this happens, someone has to come up with the extra money. The first thing you want to do is file a rebuttal with the appraiser. This is a form where you basically are trying to prove your appraisal. You will need to include comps to other properties, the repairs you did, and explanations for why your property is worth the higher price. Best case, he sees all the work you did and raises his appraisal. If not, then you have four options.

- Buyer will pay the difference with their own cash;
- Seller will drop the price;
- Buyer and seller can meet in the middle somewhere; or
- The buyer backs out of the deal.

Ideally, the buyer pays the difference since they agreed to the price, but that may not be possible. A buyer may only have enough cash for their down payment, so to ask for them to come up with more money may be hard. Either way, you want to do whatever is best for you. Don't get too caught up on forcing a deal and end up costing yourself more money.

When a Property Doesn't Sell

If your property hasn't gotten an offer after a month of being on the market, you need to ask serious questions about the listing. Are you overpriced? Have you overestimated the value of the property? Is the market slowing down? Another issue is the house. Is there something wrong with your house? Is the problem the paint color? Is the problem the layout of the house? Is there something going on in the neighborhood that is scaring potential buyers? Take time to discover and find out what is going on. You may also want to check the actual listing. Is the information accurate? Is your listing showing up on all the major sites? Check all potential issues and address any you may have. I have found that pricing is often the issue. Consult your minimum selling price and start lowering the price. Don't be too eager to lower the price, but make sure you don't end up losing profit because of high holding costs.

Another option is waiting. This is where thinking outside the box comes in handy. Remember the deal where I couldn't get the price I wanted and ended up renting the property on Airbnb for a few months. Renting it, I made more money than if I had sold it for my original price. Eventually, I was less concerned with getting the sale price I wanted because I had already made the money I would have lost renting it out.

CHAPTER 10
Failure Is an Option

I am a firm believer that people romanticize success, and nowadays with social media and influencer status, putting success on a pedestal is much easier. I am all about giving someone a nod and a round of applause for their accomplishments. But I truly believe that as a society, we spend too much time on the result of someone's successful path without spending enough time on the trials, troubles, and tribulations associated with careers and jobs. Honestly and most importantly, we need the lessons that help successfulness, which has led to becoming a high achiever. This is the reason I don't hoard knowledge. I take advantage of as many coffee dates and conversations with people eager to learn about this industry and learn about my path. I don't believe success is power. I believe the old adage that knowledge is power, and the application of that knowledge is the source of true power. I am happy to share with you some of the lessons, milestones, and miseries I've hit along my journey. These are the learning experiences and growing pains that I MUST share with you!

Failure in real estate is not just likely; it is inevitable. The good news is that it is often temporary as you learn from your mistakes and keep trying to succeed. You will have bad deals. You may even have many bad deals, at some point, losing money. You will grow discouraged. Persevering through, you can overcome. Every failure and loss gives you more knowledge so that you are smarter and wiser for your next opportunity. To maintain momentum, remember to not wallow in your disappointment or failure. Remembering the growth mindset, you will see your discrepancy as an opportunity to learn and evolve. The best way to recover from failure is by asking questions. Ask yourself, *Where did I drop the ball? What should I do next time?* When you learn from your mistakes, no level of disappointment will keep you down, and it will be the starting point for the next level of success, the stepping-stone that you need.

Balancing Risk

I mentioned it at the beginning of this book, but part of building a real estate empire is knowing how to manage risk. Taking the initial jump into full-time real estate, I had a backup plan. Yes, I was spending every dollar that I could on real estate, knowing there was the possibility that I could lose it all. However, I knew that I could take that risk because Joel had his job too. If real estate failed, we wouldn't be homeless. If real estate failed, I was still young. If real estate failed, I had a skillset that could get me right back into the workplace. We never leveraged to a point that we would lose everything if we lost a deal.

As you start growing in your real estate journey, you will be tempted to leverage to the point where you want to risk it all. Don't. Make sure at the end of the day, and this will look different for everyone, you have managed your risk to not lose it all.

Define Your Win

During your vetting processes, determine a set of benefits and expectations that are your nonnegotiables. Your nonnegotiable list will help you vet offers and opportunities that do not support best interests. There are three things every investment opportunity must offer for me to participate.

Return on Investment

This may seem obvious, but I come across deals that sound amazing, but it doesn't actually make money. Someone wanted me to partner on a project, but looking at it, it wouldn't make me any money. Sure, it would be awesome to own a mall or a twenty-million-dollar home, but if the money isn't right, it's not worth it. Like I said earlier, $25,000 is not a good return on a million-dollar investment. No matter how fun or cool a deal sounds, I only accept a project if it looks like I can get a strong ROI on it.

Control

I am not a passive investor. I like to be involved with making decisions and being in control. So even if a deal offers a great ROI, I make sure there is an active investor on the team, securing the investment. If a prospective deal meets my criteria and the two stipulations (ROI and control) will I even consider it. If it doesn't, I leave the deal on the table. If a deal doesn't meet your criteria or stipulations, you need to say no.

Pressure

There is never a need to pressure someone into making a quick decision. Yes, real estate does require speed but not pressure. If someone ever tries to pressure you into a deal, leave the meeting and stop the call as if you were leaving a burning building. When a company or person is pressuring you to quickly accept their real estate opportunity, say no and end the conversation, by leaving. The pushy car salesman approach does not work in this industry. Due diligence is necessary! Take your time! You don't have to decide in one day. Take your time and vet each opportunity. If it sounds too good, to be true it probably is! Consider by listing all pros and cons. Write out worst-case scenarios, charting how they would impact your bottom line and how they can be avoided. Make the wisest decision to the best of your ability. You are capable! Spotting and vetting good deals come with time and experience. You will learn to trust insight, data, reputation, and your intuition. Most importantly, you will learn when to walk away. Every good opportunity is not the best opportunity for you. Every opportunity that is packaged and wonderfully presented will not meet all your expectations. The ability to walk away is just as powerful as the ability to close a solid deal because doing so protects your energy, time, and money.

Conclusion

Learn to define your win through ROI, control, and pressure; you can manage your risk better. Vetting is so important. You must stick to your criteria. Stay diligent. The only time I have failed was when I had gotten greedy or overly optimistic about a deal, and greed and optimism cause investors to fail. Create your criteria. If something falls outside of it, there is probably a reason. You need to keep control of your real estate journey. People will try to pull you in different directions. They will pull you into their goals, control, pressure, or criteria. Giving in, and you have now lost control—failure may happen at any moment because you lost control. Pressure may also cause failure. When people try to control your actions by pressuring you into a deal, just stop. You are giving up control, and failure is possible. Real estate is an amazing opportunity for financial freedom; it is also an amazing opportunity to fail. Learn to manage your risk, and you will find financial freedom.

Notes: Risk and Reward

1. Defining Your Win

2. What Is Risk Tolerance? How Much Can You Afford to Lose?

CHAPTER 11

GROWING YOUR EMPIRE

Once you have sold your first house, you can begin building your empire, continuing all of the steps taken to purchase your first property. As you begin to understand the rules of real estate and start seeing cash flow coming, you will be ready to expand your real estate repertoire. In the beginning of 2021, I expanded my repertoire; my partners and I bought a hotel, a Home2Suites by Hilton in El Reno, Oklahoma. Maintaining my expectations and control through connections made in networking, I expanded into the hotel business.

Through my humble beginnings, I also built a personal brand because, at the end of the day, your success in real estate is a direct result of your personal brand. Branding is what creates familiarity with clients. Yes, having the knowledge, skills, and money helps, but the power of knowledge, skill, and money may increase exponentially if you build your brand. Suddenly, clients and contractors may begin seeking you because they want to work with you, then finding deals becomes easier.

Benefits of Building a Brand

It Expands Your Network and Builds Credibility
A strong brand will encourage people to connect with you on a personal level, making it easy to transition into either potential clients or business partners. Connecting with your audience and establishing yourself as a leader in your industry, you will build credibility. You are no longer just another person asking for money or looking to do another real estate deal; you have become a credible person, a worthwhile business partner, knowing how to manage your money.

Creating a strong branding may potentially lead to more connections. Once you are respected as an authority in your niche, you then begin to connect with other respected authority figures in your niche. Networking industry events, seminars, and conferences become a place where you share your knowledge and form potential business relationships. You will also begin to connect with people who are above you, forming relationships with others who may mentor you and encourage your real estate career.

It Boosts Confidence Levels

I once read somewhere that you only remember 5 percent of what you learn but remember 95 percent of what you teach. While sharing your knowledge with others, you are solidifying it in your own mind as well. People looking to you and viewing you as a credible source for real estate may boost your confidence, personally and professionally. For me, there is nothing better than hearing from someone who has taken my course or taken action and gained results! It always makes me stop and think, *Wow! I really know my stuff. It works for others.* As you build your confidence in yourself, others grow more confident in you as well.

It Opens Up New Opportunities to Explore

As I said at the beginning of this chapter, we bought a hotel. Six years ago, I never dreamed of owning a hotel. I was just getting started in real estate, and making $20,000 on a deal was the most incredible thing that had happened to me. Over the last few years, as I have grown my knowledge, experience, and connections, I have seen my deals grow bigger and bigger. That's no coincidence! That's the whole purpose for growing your brand—to open new opportunities. Six years ago, no one would've thought to buy a hotel with me. They certainly wouldn't have thought to sell it to me. Now, my real estate track record and connections have allowed me to buy a hotel. My partners trust and know that I am capable of making money and managing large deals. We've expanded our portfolio to include two more properties and building a resort in Exuma, Bahamas. As I continue to grow my brand, I simultaneously grow the number of opportunities available to me.

Establish Yourself as an Expert

Establishing yourself as an expert is the best way to build your brand. Experts are the go-to people in their field. For example, we think of certain billionaires (people like Grant Cardone, Elon Musk, or Jay-Z) come to mind. Of these three examples, only Elon Musk is named among the richest people in the world, yet they have one thing in common. Each of these three people have branded themselves as experts in their own fields. This expertise branding applies to a company's branding as well. Because of Apple's expertise with phones, computers, and devices, we consumers accept Apple telling us what we need to purchase and how to use our purchases. In the same way, Google can tell us where to go and where to shop; because they are branded as an expert in technology. People thinking of these individuals or companies ponder the success, innovation, influence, and branding. Success in the real estate industry requires branding and expertise.

What Does It Take to Become an Expert?

Becoming an expert does not mean you "fake it till you make it," but it does take time. Becoming an expert also has a sense of humility. Yes, you want to be seen as an expert in your field, yet at the same time, you recognize you have much to learn. There are several things you need to do to establish yourself as an expert in your field.

Be at the forefront of innovation in your industry. This does not mean falling for every new trend. It means keeping your business updated, effective, and highly efficient in real estate, innovation, and technology. For a real estate investor, this means improving the processes for buying and selling, knowing and sharing knowledge of current tax policy, and setting the standard for best practices in real estate. In fact, the devices of Apple and Google are useful tools when integrating innovative technological updates within the real estate industry. Of course, there is a balance between intuition, innovation, and discipline. Real estate investing still requires a strong sense of intuition or a "gut feeling."

Personally, I think of TikTok. Many people laughed at the idea of another social media app because it had been thought, who could break into the social media market of Facebook, Instagram, and Snapchat? Instead, innovative teenagers and businesspeople have capitalized on the creation of TikTok; they each had a "gut-feeling" of success. Innovation and intuition and discipline and continued learning will help you lead and maintain your expertise. Setting aside time to learn the real estate rules, the new devices, and online technologies will help you stay current as well as reliable as a real estate expert.

Lead by example. As an expert, you are the epitome of success in your industry. For me, I teach that real estate is the ultimate path to freedom. I truly believe that, and the proof is in my life. Just look at my life! Vacation is the constant in my life; taking cruises throughout the year and traveling around the world all show that I live what I teach, and it is possible. If your life isn't reflecting the same as what you are preaching, then you have work to do.

Have a vision. As an expert, you have a vision for the future. Steve Jobs had a vision when he founded Apple, and Bill Gates had a vision when he founded Microsoft. Each founder wanted to build a world where computers made life easier, a world that improved communications for companies and individuals, where we can access large amounts of information with the touch of a button; this was a vision that they could share with others. And they did. Jobs and Gates literally created the world that we live in today. I have a vision for real estate. In my vision, men and women can take control of their lives, escape corporate America, buy back their time, and enjoy the life they dreamed. This is the vision I share with everyone. Whether they are a man or woman, rich or poor, by following me and practicing what I teach will they experience freedom of time and finances. These freedoms will change their lives.

Experts could and should lead by example. Experts are influential enough to get people to follow them. Earning authority through branding, the expert can inspire and set a course of action for others to follow. Becoming an influential expert then leads to becoming a compelling expert, conducting a holistic analysis of best practices and then using critical analysis skills for curating better practices, initiating and encouraging change. The role of an expert is often assumed by individuals, not typically entire organizations. It is up to the organization to employ people (driven by relentless vision and a persevering spirit) who change entire business processes. Expertise is not only about coming up with groundbreaking, revolutionary ideas but includes augmenting them into a proper strategy. It is this strategy that allows people to trust and follow you.

Choose Your Platforms Wisely

Establishing yourself as an expert takes time and strategy. While looking for the best way to share your knowledge, consider how you want to share your information.

Social Media

Social media is the leading means of marketing for many businesses as well as real estate. Posting your listings for spreading the word of property, sharing your business, and sparking interest in potential buyers, social media is a perfect ingredient. Your social media posting can educate your audience about tips and tricks for buying property. Imagine doing a post on "How to Spot a Trustworthy Real Estate Agent," marketing the idea that you care about your clients. Apart from your own marketing, there are many people in the real estate industry marketing as well. Presenting the perfect opportunity to study, research, and connect with other real estate agents and investors can drastically improve your results.

Workshops

Another strategic way to network and market your business effectively is by offering free opportunities: classes or workshops for people interested in buying, selling, or investing in real estate—a useful strategy that builds trust. Classes and workshops are opportunities for expanding contacts and email lists. These free opportunities are useful for requesting feedback and reviews. It is important to identify your strengths or niche; you can market yourself within your own strength or niche. Using the internet and social media, people can search for you, in your real estate niche, and in your real estate strengths.

Websites, Radio, and Newspapers
Creating a website is a great way to house all your content, bookings, and other information. Having the best visuals on your website represents the effort you put into your market. You can get feedback using web-based programs to track the number of people visiting and clicking on your website. If you would like to expand your content or promotion beyond your website, consider including radio and newspapers. There are numerous ways to creatively market your business. Creative marketing is not easy but is worth the time. Remember, the benefits and growth of marketing and networking may not happen right away. However, be intentional, and there will be growth. Discover for yourself which of the marketing and networking ideas work best for you and maximize using it. Have fun instilling your personality while establishing your marketing identity! Your enthusiasm will affect your work and encourage your clients to work with you! The journey to establishing yourself as an expert is tiring yet worth it.

During the past few years, I have dedicated part of my day to creating content to share. Seeing my deals increase, people are contacting me to purchase my courses. Honestly, social media has become an essential tool in my business. Tips for using social media:

- Choose a platform that you are comfortable with and represents you well to your customer;

- Strive for authenticity and not perfection. Sharing what you are doing is the best way to reach your target audience; finding what works and improving it;

- Carefully observe the overarching trends that dominate your niche. Try to emulate other influencers but in your own unique way;

- Forge offline relationships in seminars and at networking events, then take them online; a great way for increasing your follower base;

- Avoid overselling yourself, of advertising yourself at every opportunity; it may cause mistrust and may sabotage your efforts to establish your credibility as a trusted expert; and

- Get published. Carve out your niche. PR is one of the best ways to build your brand awareness and establish yourself as a leader and expert in real estate.

Networking Events

I know that I have mentioned this throughout the book, but I can't stress this enough. Your next deal is always on the other side of a new connection. Sometimes we get shy sharing our dreams or successes with others. We don't want to appear over-confident, seeming like we are bragging. However, you will accelerate your growth by building your network. If someone thinks you sharing your dreams or success is bragging, you can stop sharing, but if there is someone who hears your dreams and successes, you have made a connection. You may have a new partner or client. This is the reason for networking events. Building your network and connecting with others also helps to build your brand. The more people who hear about what you do and see what you do, the more people know you, and the more people want to connect. Go network!

Develop a Niche

You don't have to limit yourself to a particular type of venture, but you will become better at your craft and able to attract a following more if you focus on a niche. In most scenarios in life, practice makes perfect. Real estate investing is not much different. Perfect your craft! Intentionally developing a depth of understanding in a specific area will set you up for success and help establish you as a trusted leader in your industry.

Encourage Referrals

Establishing a healthy business relationship and mutual respect for others is crucial to the longevity of your business. This is a two-way street. If you can share something with someone, do it! At the same time, make sure to encourage others to refer you. Word of mouth is not the fastest way to grow your brand, but it certainly is effective. If people can combine your social media presence, work, and other outlets for publicity with a personal referral, they are more than ready to do business with you.

Notes: Building Your Empire

1. Three Aspects of Becoming an Expert

2. What Is Your Greater Vision for Real Estate?

3. List of Networking to Attend

4. Potential Niche

CHAPTER 12

Conclusion

Congratulations! You have made it to the final chapter. You are now ready to go and act. No, it's not an easy process, but I promise it will all start to make sense when you go and make your first deal. When I first started in real estate, I was looking for a way to get out of corporate America. I wanted freedom to travel. I wanted control of my time. Through real estate, I have done just that. I have built a life where I can:

- Travel the world whenever I want;
- Work on my own schedule;
- Meet incredible people;
- Be my own boss; and
- Spend more time with my family.

What are your hopes for real estate? What can real estate do for you? Go ahead and write your goals on a list of paper and hang it somewhere you can see it every day. Maybe you want a side income, savings for your child's education, building a business for your family, or like I wanted, you love travel, and the thought of borrowing your own time has no appeal to you. Whatever your reasoning, real estate can provide an entrance to a new life.

Taking the information and following the steps I've given you in this book, you can transform your life. You will have all the knowledge you need to succeed. I'm not going to lie. It will take work. It doesn't happen overnight. Don't be discouraged. Be resilient. Persevere. The first deal is always the hardest, and you may lose money, but it gets easier with each deal that you make. The most important thing that I can stress is to take action. Remember, take time to network. You know the cliché, "Your network is your network"? In the real estate industry, this is 100 percent true! Invest your time going to real estate networking events, joining Facebook groups, and connecting with people, even if you must pay for your network; it's okay! The connections and knowledge you gain are well worth the price.

Another valuable shortcut to success is finding a mentor. A good mentor will save you from making costly mistakes. Vet your mentor choice as you would vet a property. Unfortunately, there are some people wanting to take your money, but

Conclusion

contracts can help you with that. On the other hand, there are good mentors with good intentions.

In addition to mentors, I encourage you to continue to learn. Check out my course *Deal MKR Academy*. This course includes the investment details and strategies I have used to build my portfolio (from wholesaling $40,000 homes to purchasing/building multi-million dollar hotels).

I have a very active community online. Please follow me on IG @itsJessicaMyers or my website itsjessicamyers.com.

As always, you know you got it. Let's get it, let's goooooooooo!

Eight Steps to Real Estate Success

1. Build Your Criteria;
2. Build Your Team;
3. Start Networking and Find Your First Deal;
4. Buy Your First House;
5. Renovate Your First House;
6. Share Your Journey on Social Media;
7. Continue to Network and Learn; and
8. Rinse and Repeat.

Contract Templates

LEASE AGREEMENT

I. THE PARTIES. This Lease Agreement ("Agreement") made this _____,20 is between:

Landlord: _____, with a mailing address of ("Landlord"), AND

Tenant(s); _____, with a mailing address of
_____("Tenant").

NOW, THEREFORE, FOR AND IN CONSIDERATION of the mutual promises and agreements contained herein, the Tenant agrees to lease the Premises from the Landlord under the following terms and conditions:

II. LEASE TYPE. This Agreement shall be considered a: (check one)

☐ **-Fixed Lease**. The Tenant shall be allowed to occupy the Premises starting on _____, 20, and end on _____,20 ("Lease Term"). At the end of the Lease Term and no renewal is made, the Tenant: (check one)

☐ - May continue to lease the Premises under the same terms of this Agreement under a month-to-month arrangement

☐ - Must vacate the Premises.

☐ **- Month-to-Month Lease**. The Tenant shall be allowed to occupy the Premises on a month-to-month arrangement starting on _____. 20____and ending upon notice of____days from either the Landlord or Tenant ("Lease Term").

III. PAYMENT TERMS. During the Lease Term, the Tenant shall be responsible for the following: (check all that apply)

☐ **- Monthly Rent:** $_____ due on the_____ of each month.

☐ **- Security Deposit:** $_____ due at signing of this Agreement

☐ **- Last Month's Rent:** $_____ due at signing of this Agreement.

☐ -_____: $_____ due _____.

☐ -_____: $_____ due _____.

☐ -_____: $_____ due _____.

IV. UTILITIES. The Tenant shall be responsible for all utilities and services to the Premises except for:
_____

V. OTHER TERMS. _____
_____
_____

Landlord's Signature: _____ Tenant's Signature: _____

Print Name: _____ Print Name: _____

Standard Purchase and Sale Agreement

This agreement is made this _____ day of _____, 20_____

Between Seller (s) _____

And Buyer(s)_____ and/ or assigns.

Seller agrees to sell, and buyer agrees to buy the following described real property together with all improvements and fixtures and the personal property described below:

Street Address _____

City, State, Zip: _____

Legal description: _____

The purchase price to be paid as follows:

Earnest Money Deposit	$_____
Cash to Seller at Closing	$_____
Total Purchase Price	$_____

1. EARNEST MONEY to be deposited with a licensed title company or attorney within 48 hours of acceptance and ratification of offer. If this contract is canceled by buyer pursuant to the terms of this contract, buyer becomes entitled to a return of the EMD and escrow agent shall immediately refund to buyer all EMD then in escrow.

2. FINANCING: Funds to purchase this property shall be:

_____Cash. 'Cash' is defined as capital from buyer's personal funds and/or buyer's investors, partners and/or unconventional lending sources. This agreement is not contingent on buyer securing funds to close.

_____Seller Financing with the following terms: _____

3. PRORATIONS, IMPOUNDS & SECURITY DEPOSITS: Loan interest, property taxes, insurance, and rents shall be prorated as of the date of closing. All security deposits shall be transferred to buyer at closing. Alim pound accounts for taxes and insurance are included in the purchase price and shall be transferred to buyer at closing. Any shortage in these accounts shall be charged to seller at closing.

4. CLOSING DATE AND TRANSFER OF TITLE: This transaction shall close on or before:

_____, 20____ Closing will be held at _____ and Seller(s) agree to transfer marketable title free and clear of all encumbrances except those listed and pay any required state taxes or stamps required to record deed and mortgage. Seller agrees to furnish title insurance in the amount of the purchase price, showing no encumbrances or exceptions other than previously noted.

BUYER(S) INITIALS _____   SELLER(S) INITIALS _____

5. ESCROW AND CLOSING FEES: Closing fees due at close of escrow with the exception of delinquent property taxes, mortgage liens, mechanics liens, IRS liens, judgements and/or any liens to be paid as follows:

_____Buyer and Seller shall each pay their respective escrow and closing fees according to the usual and customary practices in the state of _____

_____Buyer and Seller agree to split evenly all escrow and closing costs.

_____Buyer shall pay all escrow and closing fees

_____Seller shall pay all escrow and closing fees.

6. DAMAGE TO PROPERTY: Seller shall maintain property in its current condition and keep it insured against all loss until closing. In the event of destruction covered by insurance, buyer may elect to close and collect the insurance proceeds.

7. INSPECTION PERIOD: Buyer's obligations to close this transaction are subject to the satisfaction of buyer's inspections and investigations of the property. Buyer shall have until the business day before close of escrow (the "inspection period"), during which time Buyer will have the absolute right to cancel this contract for any reason whatsoever at buyer's sole and absolute discretion. Upon such cancellation, buyer shall be entitled to a return of all earnest money held in escrow. Unless buyer gives written notice of cancellation before the expiration date of the inspection period, then buyer will be deemed to have elected not to cancel this contract.

8. ACCESS TO PROPERTY: Between contract date and close of escrow, seller grants buyer and/or buyer's employees, inspectors, partners, investors, contractors and/or agent(s) full access to the property as follows:

_____**VACANT**. If the property is vacant as of the contract date, buyer reserves the right to install a lockbox on the property, which will contain a key to the property supplied by the seller. Seller acknowledges and agrees that the lockbox will permit access to the property, and that it is possible an unauthorized person may go into the property. Buyer is not insuring seller against theft, loss or vandalism resulting from any unauthorized access

_____**OCCUPIED.** If the property is occupied by seller, tenant or otherwise as of the contract date, seller will permit the buyer access with a 24-hour notice.

9. TENANT OCCUPIED. If the property is used as a rental property, tenant shall:

_____Vacate property before the close of escrow.

_____Continue occupying property according to applicable and current lease agreement. Seller shall deliver the following to buyer within five days of contract date: (a) current lease(s) of the property: (b) a certified rent roll (which seller will update at least five days before close of escrow); (c) evidence of security deposits on hand, if any.

10. PROPERTY TURNOVER. Seller will provide buyer the keys to the property at closing of escrow.

BUYER(S) INITIALS_____   SELLER(S) INITIALS _____

11. DEBRIS/PERSONAL BELONGINGS. At close of escrow, seller shall deliver the property to buyer:

_____WITH debris and/or personal belongings that are currently present in the property. Buyer assumes all responsibility for trash-out, removal and clean-up of said debris/belongings from the interior/exterior of the property.

_____WITHOUT debris and/or personal belongings that are currently present in the property. Seller assumes all responsibility for trash-out, removal and clean-up of said debris/belongings from the interior/exterior of the property.

12. ADDITIONAL PERSONAL PROPERTY. The following personal property is to be included in the sale herein: if any: _____

13. INVESTOR DISCLOSURE. Seller acknowledges that buyer is an investor and purchases properties with the intent to lease, "flip", resell, or otherwise make a profit. Seller acknowledges that the purchase price may be less than market value, and is willingly selling it as such for convenience, to save time, lack of funds to renovate/update, and/or other personal reasons. Seller waives any claims against any existing equity or added value arising from the property. Buyers has not made seller any representations or promises as to the value of the property in its "as-is" condition.

14. LEAD BASED PAINT ACKNOWLEDGEMENT: All parties acknowledge that residential dwellings constructed prior to 1978 are likely to contain lead-based paint which could create a health hazard. In the event that the real property which is the subject of this agreement consists of or contains a residential unit built prior to 1978, the parties agree that each party has received, reviewed, signed and annexed hereto a completed disclosure and acknowledgment form regarding lead-based paint as required by federal HUD/EPA disclosure regulations.

15. REPRESENTATIONS BY SELLER. Seller represents and warrants to buyer as follows: (a) Seller has no actual knowledge and has received no notice that the property is not in compliance withal applicable laws governing the use and operation thereof, nor, to sellers actual knowledge, does there exist any facts or circumstances on the property which notice or the passage of time would constitute such violation. (b) As of contract date, seller has not entered into any other agreements or contracts to sell the property. (c) Seller has disclosed to buyer all material latent defects and any information concerning the properly known to seller.

16. OTHER AGREEMENTS. Seller shall not enter into an agreement or contract to purchase with anyone else concerning the property from and after the contract date. Should seller participate in another agreement which will interfere with close of escrow, seller will be responsible for any and all costs and losses to buyer.

17. AGENCY. Seller acknowledges they have not been represented by the buyer or by any representative of the buyer with respect to the purchase and sale of the property. Seller agrees and understands that the buyer and any buyer's representative are not acting as seller's broker or agent in the transaction and have been acting solely for buyer's own benefit as a principle to this agreement. Seller agrees to hold buyer free from any/all liability regarding the property and transaction arising from any claims of agency.

18. ASSIGNMENT AND RELEASE. Seller agrees and acknowledges that buyer may assign their rights under this agreement to a wholly or partially owned entity of the buyer or third party that will close directly with the seller. If such an assignment should happen, seller agrees to release buyer from any liability or duties under this agreement.

BUYER(S) INITIALS _____   SELLER(S) INITIALS_____

19. RIGHT TO COUNSEL. Seller represents and agrees that seller fully understands seller's rights to discuss all aspects of this contract with an attorney, that seller has carefully read and fully understands all of the provisions of this contract. That seller freely and voluntarily entered into this contract and seller has read this document in its entirety and fully understands the meaning, intent and consequences of this contract. This representation will survive this contract's termination.

20. GOVERNING LAW|JURISDICTION. This agreement shall be governed by, construed, and enforced under the laws of the state of _____whose courts shall have jurisdiction over any legal proceedings or actions arising out of this agreement. _____County, in the **state of** _____ shall be the place of venue of any such proceeding or action.

19. ADDITIONAL TERMS AND CONDITIONS: (If none write none)
_____
_____
_____
_____

The undersigned have read the above information, understand it and verify that it is correct.

Seller: Seller:

    Signature   Date   Signature   Date

    Printed Name   Printed Name

Buyer: Buyer:

    Signature   Date   Signature   Date

    Printed Name   Printed Name

Disclosure of Information on Lead-Based Paint and/or Lead-Based Paint Hazards

Lead Warning Statement

Housing built before 1978 may contain lead-based paint. Lead from paint, paint chips, and dust can pose health hazards if not managed properly. Lead exposure is especially harmful to young children and pregnant women. Before renting pre-1978 housing, lessors must disclose the presence of known lead-based paint and/or lead-based paint hazards in the dwelling. Lessees must also receive a federally approved pamphlet on lead poisoning prevention.

Lessor's Disclosure

(a) Presence of lead-based paint and/or lead-based paint hazards (check (1) or (ii) below):

(i) ____ Known lead-based paint and/or lead-based paint hazards are present in the housing (explain)
_____

(ii) ____ Lessor has no knowledge of lead-based paint and/or lead-based paint hazards in the housing

(b) Records and reports available to the lessor (check (i) or (ii) below):

(i) ____ Lessor has provided the lessee with all available records and reports pertaining to lead-based paint and/or lead-based paint hazards in the housing (list documents below).
_____
_____

(ii) ____ Lessor has no reports or records pertaining to lead-based paint and/or lead-based paint hazards in the housing,

Lessee's Acknowledgment (initial)

(c)_____ Lessee has received copies of all information listed above.

(d) _____ Lessee has received the pamphlet *Protect Your Family from Lead in Your Home.*

Agent's Acknowledgment (initial)

(e)_____ Agent has informed the lessor of the lessor's obligations under 42 U.S.C. 4852d and is aware of his/her responsibility to ensure compliance.

Certification of Accuracy The following parties have reviewed the information above and certify, to the best of their knowledge, that the information they have provided is true and accurate.

Lessor	Date	Lessor	Date
Lessee	Date	Lessee	Date
Agent	Date	Agent	Date

DURABLE FINANCIAL POWER OF ATTORNEY

On the___ day of_____ ,20____ I, _____ , the principal, of _____ ,State of _____ , hereby designate _____ ,of _____ State of _____ , my attorney-in-fact (hereinafter my "attorney-in-fact"), to act as initialed below, in my name, in my stead and for my benefit, hereby revoking any and all financial powers of attorney I may have executed in the past.

EFFECTIVE DATE

(Choose the applicable paragraph by placing your initials in the preceding space)

_____ - A. I grant my attorney-in-fact the powers set forth herein immediately upon the execution of this document. These powers shall not be affected by any subsequent disability or incapacity I may experience in the future.

or

_____ - B. I grant my attorney-in-fact the powers set forth herein only when it has been determined in writing, by my attending physician, that I am unable to properly handle my financial affairs.

POWERS OF ATTORNEY-IN-FACT

My attorney-in-fact shall exercise powers in my best interests and for my welfare, as a fiduciary. My attorney-in-fact shall have the following powers:

(Choose the applicable power(s) by placing your initials in the preceding space)

_____**BANKING** - To receive and deposit funds in any financial institution, and to withdraw funds by check or otherwise to pay for goods, services, and any other personal and business expenses for my benefit. If necessary to affect my attorney-in fact's powers, my attorney-in-fact is authorized to execute any document required to be signed by such banking institution.

_____**SAFE DEPOSIT BOX** - To have access at any time or times to any safe deposit box rented by me or to which I may have access, wheresoever located, including drilling, if necessary, and to remove all or any part of the contents thereof, and to surrender or relinquish said safe-deposit box; and any institution in which any such safe-deposit box may be located shall not incur any liability to me or my estate as a result of permitting my attorney-in-fact to exercise this power.

_____ **LENDING OR BORROWING** - To make loans in my name; to borrow money in my name, individually or jointly with others; to give promissory notes or other

obligations therefor; and to deposit or mortgage as collateral or for security for the payment thereof any or all of my securities, real estate, personal property, or other property of whatever nature and wherever situated, held by me personally or in trust for my benefit.

_____ **GOVERNMENT BENEFITS** - To apply for and receive any government benefits for which I may be eligible or become eligible, including but not limited to, Social Security, Medicare and Medicaid.

_____ **RETIREMENT PLAN** - To contribute to select payment option of, roll-over, and receive benefits of any retirement plan or IRAI may own, except my attorney-in-fact shall not have power to change the beneficiary of any of my retirement plans or IRAs.

_____ **TAXES** - To complete and sign any local, state and federal tax returns on my behalf, pay any taxes and assessments due and receive credits and refunds owed to me and to sign any tax agency documents necessary to effectuate these powers.

_____**INSURANCE** - To purchase, pay premiums and make claims on life, health, automobile and homeowners' insurance on my behalf, except my attorney-in-fact shall not have the power to cash in or change the beneficiary of any life insurance policy.

_____**REAL ESTATE** - To acquire, purchase, exchange, lease, grant options to sell, and sell and convey real property, or any interests therein, on such terms and conditions, including credit arrangements, as my attorney-in-fact shall deem proper; to execute, acknowledge and deliver, under seal or otherwise, any and all assignments, transfers, deeds, papers, documents or instruments which my attorney-in-fact shall deem necessary in connection therewith.

_____**PERSONAL PROPERTY** - To acquire, purchase, exchange, lease, grant options to sell, and sell and convey personal property, or any interests therein, on such terms and conditions, including credit arrangements, as my attorney-in-fact shall deem proper; to execute, acknowledge and deliver, under seal or otherwise, any and all assignments, transfers, titles, papers, documents or instruments which my attorney-in fact shall deem necessary in connection therewith; to purchase, sell or otherwise dispose of, assign, transfer and convey shares of stock, bonds, securities and other personal property now or hereafter belonging to me, whether standing in my name or otherwise, and wherever situated.

_____**POWER TO MANAGE PROPERTY**- To maintain, repair, improve, invest, manage, insure, rent, lease, encumber, and in any manner deal with any real or personal property, tangible or intangible, or any interests therein, that I now own or may hereafter acquire, in my name and for my benefit, upon such terms and conditions as my attorney-in-fact shall deem proper.

_____**GIFTS** - To make gifts, grants, or other transfers (including the forgiveness of indebtedness and the completion of any charitable pledges I may have made) without consideration, either outright or in trust to such person(s) (including my attorney-in-fact hereunder) or organizations as my attorney-in-fact shall select, including, without limitation, the following actions: (a) transfer by gift in advancement of a bequest or devise to beneficiaries under my will or in the absence of a will to my spouse and descendants in whatever degree, and (b) release of any life interest, or waiver, renunciation, disclaimer, or declination of any gift to me by will, deed, or trust

_____**LEGAL ADVICE AND PROCEEDINGS** - To obtain and pay for legal advice, to initiate or defend legal and administrative proceedings on my behalf, including actions against third parties who refuse, without cause,to honor this instrument.

SPECIAL INSTRUCTIONS: On the following lines are any special instructions limiting or extending the powers I give to my attorney-in-fact (Write "None" if no additional instructions are given):

_____
_____
_____
_____

AUTHORITY OF ATTORNEY-IN-FACT: Any party dealing with my attorney-in-fact hereunder may rely absolutely on the authority granted herein and need not look to the application of any proceeds nor the authority of my attorney-in-fact as to any action taken hereunder. In this regard, no person who may in good faith act in reliance upon the representations of my attorney-in-fact or the authority granted hereunder shall incur any liability to me or my estate as a result of such act. I hereby ratify and confirm whatever my attorney-in-fact shall lawfully do under this instrument. My attorney-in-fact is authorized as he or she deems necessary to bring an action in court so that this instrument shall be given the full power and effect that I intend on by executing it.

LIABILITY OF ATTORNEY-IN-FACT: My attorney-in-fact shall not incur any liability to me under this power except for a breach of fiduciary duty.

REIMBURSEMENT OF ATTORNEY-IN-FACT: My attorney-in-fact is entitled to reimbursement for reasonable expenses incurred in exercising powers hereunder, and to reasonable compensation for services provided as attorney-in-fact.

AMENDMENT AND REVOCATION: I can amend or revoke this power of attorney through a writing delivered to my attorney-in-fact. Any amendment or revocation is ineffective as to a third party until such third party has notice of such revocation or amendment.

STATE LAW: This Power of Attorney is governed by the laws of the State of _____.

PHOTOCOPIES: Photocopies of this document can be relied upon as though they were originals.

IN WITNESS WHEREOF, I have on this _____ day of _____, 20_____. executed this Financial Power of Attorney.

_____
Principal's Signature

We, the witnesses, each do hereby declare in the presence of the principal that the principal signed and executed this instrument in the presence of each of us, that the principal signed it willingly, that each of us hereby signs this Power of Attorney as witness at the request of the principal and in the principal's presence, and that, to the best of our knowledge, the principal is eighteen years of age or over, of sound mind, and under no constraint or undue influence.

_____
Witness's Signature

_____
Address

_____
Witness's Signature

_____
Address

STATE OF _____

_____County, ss.

On this_____ day of _____, 20, before me appeared _____ as Principal of this Power of Attorney who proved to me through government issued photo identification to be the above-named person, in my presence executed foregoing instrument and acknowledged that (s)he executed the same as his/her free act and deed.

_____
Notary Public

My commission expires: _____

SPECIMEN SIGNATURE AND ACCEPTANCE OF APPOINTMENT

I, _____, the attorney-in-fact named above, hereby accept appointment as attorney-in-fact in accordance with the foregoing instrument.

_____
Attorney-in-Fact's Signature

STATE OF _____

_____County, ss.

On this _____day of _____, 20_____, before me appeared _____ as Attorney-in-Fact of this Power of Attorney who proved to me through government issued photo identification to be the above-named person, in my presence executed the foregoing acceptance of appointment and acknowledged that (s)he executed the same as his/her free act and deed.

_____
Notary Public

My commission expires: _____

SIMPLE CONTRACT

This Contract is entered into by and between _____ [AN INDIVIDUAL, OR TYPE OF BUSINESS ENTITY] ("First Party"), and _____, [AN INDIVIDUAL, OR TYPE OF BUSINESS ENTITY] ("Second Party"). The term of this Agreement shall begin on [BEGIN DATE] and shall continue through its termination date of [END DATE].

The specific terms of this Contract are as follows:

1.

2.

3.

In consideration of the mutual promises set forth herein, the First Party covenants and agrees that it shall_____
_____
_____

The Second Party covenants and agrees that it shall_____
_____
_____

This Contract may not be modified in any manner unless in writing and signed by both parties. This document and any attachments hereto constitute the entire agreement between the Parties. This Contract shall be binding upon the Parties, their successors, heirs and assigns and shall be enforced under the laws of the State of _____.

_____   _____
(Signature)   (Signature)

_____   _____
(Printed Name)   (Printed Name)

_____   _____
(Address)   (Address)

Date:_____,20__   Date: _____, 20_____

CPSIA information can be obtained
at www.ICGtesting.com
Printed in the USA
JSHW080833051122
32563JS00012B/11